The Pranks An' Enlightenment of
Frank An' Me

By Robert Wolley

Copyright 1997 Robert Wolley

All characters are fictitious.

All rights reserved. For permission to reprint or reproduce any part of this book, please contact the author or the publisher.

ISBN #: 1-884707-49-1

Published by
Lifestyles Press
P.O. Box 1140
Tavares, FL 32778
(352) 742-2155

**Cover art and interior illustrations by Mark Adams
Cover design by Ronnie Mesa**

*For Carolyn, my granddaughter,
who liked the first stories so much
and who cajoled me into completing
this book.*

TABLE OF CONTENTS

Chapter I	Frank	1
Chapter II	Some of the Captains an' Their Boats	18
Chapter III	Cloyd, The Rumrunners an' the Sheep	43
Chapter IV	The Model A, The "Deathmobile" an' the Buick	55
Chapter V	Party Lines	65
Chapter VI	Some Smalltown Folks	83
Chapter VII	When Frank an' Me Were Men	106
Chapter VIII	Between Bein' Child an' Man	122
Chapter IX	Rumrunnin' Alice	145
Chapter X	Some Navigation	161
Chapter XI	Jess Potter: "It's a no go, Moe"	173
Chapter XII	The Fine Arts	185
	An' Finally	211

Robert Wolley

Chapter I

Frank

The Pranks An' Enlightenment of Frank An' Me

That Frank, always full of ideas. Now he had come up with a new one, a get-rich scheme which for ten year olds could mean a pile of pennies. Back then pennies were real money, hard cash, and actually bought things. Eleven cents bought a gallon of gasoline; even one bought a handful of hard candy; five bought a cream soda or a root beer. Pennies were not to be sniffed at.

Because there were several ice houses on Long Pond and several ice cutters, there was a dispute that winter over who owned the ice. The winter was particularly warm, which made what ice there was especially valuable. Apparently, when the ice became thick enough to cut, and there was only one cutting that year, arguments broke out, then fistfighting over the little clear ice available. It all ended up in court.

Naturally, in tiny Smalltown, the squabble got played out in the town as well. Frank's pa was of the opinion that no one owned the ice, that "first come, first served," that "to him that hath shall be given," and a bunch of other proverbs that Frank's pa was given to quote, not the least of which was that "possession is nine-tenths of the law."

For some reason Frank kept reciting the proverbs, especially the "first come" and "possession" words. That winter we had been studying the expansion of the colonies and how men had come to the Cape "to worship God and to make money," or maybe it was the other way around, and about buying land from the Indians and about King's Grants and the Plymouth Colonial Court granting land rights.

Frank's pa was one of Smalltown's assessors and the fence viewer and a couple of other things, all small, part-time jobs which paid hardly anything but which, added to his government pension, allowed Frank's family to survive. Frank's pa had been crippled in the First World War.

When the ice question came up, we learned about lots of land in Smalltown that had no owners, the salt marshes particularly. Once they had been important holdings when cattle were raised, but except for a cow or two, no cattle herds had been in Smalltown for a hundred years.

"No one owns that land?" Frank asked his pa.

"Guess the town does, but it ain't been on the books since I know of."

Frank's pa went on to say that the tax records had been lost in the 1869 fire and no one had ever claimed to own certain marshes, probably because they would be liable for taxes if they did.

"What about the other stuff?" Frank pressed.

"Thousands of acres, lots of it scrub pine and oak; no owners. Wish we knew who owned it. Town needs the money."

And that was how Frank inveigled me into the real estate business. According to Frank's idea, we'd sell the land, get paid for selling it, and make a fortune.

We left Frank's pa shaking his head.

We didn't know that anybody could have had the land almost for the asking, if they had the means to pay the taxes, and not back taxes, either, just the current ones. The land was worthless or virtually so.

But Frank's enthusiasm enticed me, and we plowed ahead. We appropriated paper from school and spent several afternoons preparing posters which we hung all over town, offering land we didn't own to people who couldn't afford even the 25 cents an acre we had decided to ask. To make matters more ridiculous, we didn't even know what an acre was.

People thought the idea was "cute." How I hated that word. I didn't want to be cute; I wanted to be rich, although my being rich at that time meant having a few pennies jingling in my pocket.

Naturally, nothing came of the enterprise. A couple of the old fishermen called us "purveyors." I tried to find that word in Gran'ma's dictionary, but I couldn't because I spelled it with an "e." Frank's pa finally set us straight, and when I said that we

The Pranks An' Enlightenment of Frank An' Me

weren't supplying anything, he laughed and said that yes we were; we were supplying everyone with a good joke. While I guess we did, I've always been a bit tender about it. Frank's was an honest-to-goodness fine idea, except that we were years ahead of our time. Land that could have been bought then for a few dollars now costs hundreds of thousands, and is rarely available.

I had only one friend, really. Frank. The plain truth is that Frank and I were each other's only friend because in Smalltown when we were growing up there were no others our age, not even girls.

I don't know what we would have done if we had not liked each other. Just thinking about that situation makes me sad. But we did like each other, thank the Lord A'mighty for that, and we were as close as any two people could get, even when we had disagreements. Lordy, could we disagree, but always we came to an understanding, one way or another, and always we were best friends.

People used to say we were close because there was no one else, but we knew that just wasn't so. We were friends because we wanted to be.

Frank and I were born just three days apart. Lots of people would ask us if we weren't twins. That was unlikely, even if they were teasing us, because Frank had black hair and brown eyes and was naturally tanned, since some of his family came to the Cape from Portugal a long time ago, whereas I was light and blue-eyed and blond, my ancestors coming from England and Scotland.

According to Frank's ma, only Frank's two sets of great gran'parents were pure Portuguese, his gran'parents marrying other nationalities, and their children, too. Frank carries some of the Portuguese darkness but only when compared to me. That and his curly dark black hair was about all that set us apart.

Robert Wolley

I didn't get to Smalltown until I was three weeks old because my ma got caught off Cape when my time came, so I was not Cape born, although when I was a youngster, Cape Cod ancestor-snobbery was little known; that attitude blossomed sometime after the Second World War when the Cape exploded as a retirement and tourist place.

During my and Frank's growing up years, as it had been for so long, Smalltown was an isolated, tiny place of about two hundred and fifty people, maybe a fifth of whom were of Portuguese descent. Most of the Portuguese men had come to work on the fishing boats. Several of the men were owners of their own boats. A few had come, or their great gran'parents had, by way of the whaling ships, but most had drifted down from New Bedford and Fall River and Gloucester. All of the Portuguese families had been in Smalltown a long while. Nobody ever came to Smalltown looking for work; there was not enough work to go around as it was; such were the meager prospects for the town. I cannot recall there ever being an instance when one's parentage or heritage was mentioned. If there had been distinctions drawn, as undoubtedly there were, it was before Frank and I were born and long since forgotten.

The two things I remember most vividly are contrary things: how little most of us had and how blessedly happy I was to be alive in Smalltown.

"Poor" and "happy" would be considered a contradiction today. And before I give the wrong impression, I never knew that we were poor. I don't think I ever heard that word applied to our condition. One might be in poor health or one might speak of poor Josh, but that was because Josh had suffered some kind of loss or tragedy. We had a roof, and food and clothing — we even had an automobile — and we had many a good time, and for the most part we enjoyed our lives as they were.

The Pranks An' Enlightenment of Frank An' Me

Oh, there were bad, terrible times, too. Pa's leaving us; that was the worst. And when Frank died; never in my life was I able to get that tragedy out of my mind. And when Gran'ma died, because until she did, I didn't know that she had been holding everything together. As the old hymns she liked to sing said, she was the tie that binds; she was the rock, to mix metaphors.

It has been said: "Any man who would go to sea for pleasure would go to hell for pastime." Smalltown was a fishing port, had been from the beginning; what went on, in and under the seas was its only business; anything else was secondary to that. The sea had claimed its share; Smalltown had scores of "widows" whose husbands would never return. Husbands, fathers, brothers, and sons are remembered with granite monuments; more recently, daughters and sisters are remembered, too. The sea is friend and foe; it gives less easily than it takes, and when it takes there is a somber bleakness on the land, even as men and women set sail to wrest their livelihood from the unforgiving water.

However profound the losses, those who are born to the sea respect it but do not fear it the way landlubbers do. I fear roller coasters, yet I see city kids riding on them with no more thought than they give to buses. They, as I did, think only of their invincibility.

So it was with Frank and me. Commercial fishing was our natural goal. I don't believe that either of us was conscious of the fact that the sea offered our only way of life, although it did, or that we were inexorably guided in that direction by forces too subtle to be recognized even by the people who were a part of the force.

Our growing up time was a precious time because it was the comedy (as in classical Greek *kōmōidia*) before the tragedy. Frank and I made life comic, Frank especially. We approached our world as two cubs might; everything was new and mysterious and awaited our unique touch.

For instance, the first day the first year we went to school. I didn't like it much, and perhaps that was why I had to go to the necessary so soon. Miss Bennett, who would be our teacher for the first two years, kept pushing me back in my seat. There were four or five boys in the class and a few more girls, and I got all the boys to demand that we go, so finally Miss Bennett had to take us.

The necessary was no more than a sink at the end of the hall. She lined us up and pulled a curtain, and everyone made a little puddle that ran ever so slowly to the hole. I never had seen that before.

But making water was not what I was about. I couldn't see a seat or a big hole, but down came my sails, and I balanced on the edge of the sink. Frank and the others were laughing about as hard as they could. That got Miss Bennett's attention, and she pulled back the curtain.

There I was, sails at my ankles, legs dangling in mid-air, my doings in the sink. Miss Bennett nearly fainted. Maybe she did. I'm not sure because I covered my eyes.

But just as plain, so I remember it now, Frank asked, "'Cuse us, Miss Bennett, could we's have a bit o' paper?"

Now if that weren't enough, the boys' laughter and Miss Bennett's screaming got the girls' attention, and they came out of the classroom door and spied me, legs still dangling, sails all furled around my boot tops.

Zap went the curtain, and between laughs, we were all yelling for paper. It didn't come, but finally Frank fetched some.

I had let some mess in the sink, and it didn't go down the hole. I didn't know what to do, but lack of knowledge didn't last long. Miss Bennett regained her senses, tried to help me raise my britches, and gave my ear such a twist that to this day I believe

The Pranks An' Enlightenment of Frank An' Me

it is bigger than the other one. She gave me a mop and a pail, showed me the water supply, and directed my now undivided and shameful attention to the outhouse behind the town hall.

Thank the Lord she was a forgiving woman, more forgiving than some of the girls who for a long time remembered seeing me in a compromising posture.

And Frank never forgot it. A few years later in school, he wrote a poem referring to it. I can't remember it verbatim, except the last line, which angered me: "An' the big girls ask if he's still a little boy," with the emphasis on little.

One morning in the third grade, I got to school before the others. It was winter and the stove in the back of our classroom was going. Above the stove in the ceiling was a large hole covered by an iron grate because the second floor was used as a sometime office and as a storeroom for the town hall and because the classroom stove provided all the heat for the upstairs. I had gone into the classroom because it was cold outdoors and was just waiting for activities to begin when something struck my back. I looked around; no one was there. Then: *whack* again. And then, *splat* on the blackboard. I saw the biggest spitball I had ever seen.

When I heard the grate rattle, I looked up and there was Frank's face grinning down on me. About that time in came the teacher and the others. I figured Frank would crawl down on the stairs, but he stayed put. As Miss Rogers was taking attendance, a wad of paper splattered on the board behind her. Either she didn't hear it or she elected to ignore it; I don't know which. But when she missed the second one, there was no containing the students.

Miss Rogers gave us the glance of the devil himself. We all looked down at our desks. *Splat.* When we looked up, Miss Rogers was wearing a spitball on her chest, and she was fit to be tied. Did you ever want to laugh so hard your belly and bladder ached and at the same time have to look so innocent that angels would be jealous? Well, that was how it was with us.

Miss Rogers believed it was one of the boys. Naturally, she held the girls blameless. And since the only boys that day were John Paine and I, it had to be one or both of us.

Miss Rogers planned her reaction well. She had the girls stand. Then she marched them next door to Miss Bennett's classroom. She came back to whip John and me until we confessed.

While Miss Rogers was gone, I opened up the top of the stove and threw in all the paper and stuff I could. The fire grew rapidly, hot and dangerous. At least Miss Rogers thought so when she came back.

But so did Frank. He was forced to leave his perch, and when he did, Miss Rogers caught him and punished him good and proper.

First, she took the belt off his pants. Then she made Frank drop his pants, and in front of his classmates, he had to bend over. Then, with his own belt, mind you, she laid into him.

I don't know how many times she hit him, only three or four probably, but it was a lesson, one especially humiliating to Frank but not lost on him or us. You must remember that punishment like that was not only allowed but encouraged, especially for the times and in sea towns like ours. Many a seaman was whipped on shipboard who might have done differently had he been whipped in school.

Frank never cried. When Miss Rogers was finished, I never forgot this, she got on her knees and hugged Frank, tears coming down her cheeks. I think she had to give the lesson, but the punishment was harder on her. And she never said anything to Frank's parents, although they knew about it that day.

Later that year, in the spring, I got whipped by Miss Rogers. My crime was swearing in the schoolyard, only my punishment was done privately. We were having recess. For some reason which I have long forgotten, I uttered some forbidden words. I remember that I was guilty, so I had to accept the consequences.

Miss Rogers grabbed hold of me and dragged me back into the classroom. Since I admitted freely that I had shouted the nasty words, she gave me choice of punishment. I could take the usual physical punishment: whipping, or I could have my mouth washed out with soap. I chose the soap.

When I had suffered that indignity, Miss Rogers asked me if I had learned my lesson.

"You're g.d. right," I blurted out. Oh, no; I had done it again.

Miss Rogers stretched up to her full height. "Your belt, please." She sure was angry.

And when I told her that I didn't have a belt, her anger turned to wrath. She search the classroom for a ruler, found one, and had me bend over. She struck me several times, but maybe in the emotion of the moment, she had forgotten to have me drop my pants. The blows were painless but I winced each time she landed one just to keep up the appearance of being punished.

When she had exhausted herself, she held my face in her hands, tears falling down her sleeves. "I have no heart for this business," she said, but I don't think she was talking to me, more likely to herself. After a couple of minutes she let me go, after I had pledged to speak no more foul words.

Nothing more was said about that instance of discipline; no report was ever made to Ma. It was a private event between teacher and student. Only a series of misconducts would result in home report.

Such capital punishment is outlawed today for good and sufficient reasons. So are hugging and comforting a child as Miss Rogers touched me. If punishment is given with the intent to give harm, then it is hideously wrong. I never saw or heard of that kind of punishment in my schools; if our "crimes" were particularly serious, we expected to receive the appropriate consequences, and the consequences were delivered to get our attention, not to harm us, and once the crime/punishment sequence was completed, no more was done or said, unless, of course, the misconduct was repeated.

Our people were of a long seafaring tradition and discipline was a part of that tradition. No one knows better than sailors how important conduct and discipline can be, and if we could not discipline ourselves, we had to expect that others would do it for us.

Recent developments have stripped teachers of one of their most powerful tools — touch. Touching a student today seems to imply a perversion. There was no such implication when Miss Rogers hugged Frank or when she touched my face. She was giving comfort and support in a way that goes back to the very beginning of animal life. She was demonstrating an empathy that was essential in preserving our society; she was making a statement about the connection between generations; she was reinforcing her authority with love for the child even as she disapproved of that child's behavior. There was nothing sinister or untoward about the act of touching. We had done wrong; our conduct needed correcting; we were still loved, even more so because we had it in our powers now to improve.

And it is amazing how a touch could change a situation. Many a potentially disastrous situation was disarmed simply by a teacher's touch; many times a student's anger was softened by a simple touch on the arm or shoulder; many times sympathy or understanding was conveyed in a touch.

All our teachers were good ladies, although at the time we sometimes held other opinions. It did not seem natural for such free spirits to be penned up all day long. Miss Rogers went off the next year to get married, and Miss Bennett, who was old, retired sometime after that. Neither was replaced when she left because there were no children to fill the desks.

The Pranks An' Enlightenment of Frank An' Me

Frank and I were in the sixth grade, I think, when those that came to Smalltown from Pilot finally had their own school, and the few of us left had the same teacher, Miss Barney, and the same classroom when it finally came down to just the six of us, Frank and the Chambers girls and me. When Miss Barney had to leave, we had many different teachers for a spell.

I cannot remember not working. There was some work for boys willing to do odd jobs, and the pennies helped at home for certain.

I had Miss Harper's groceries to carry on Friday afternoons. Saturday mornings I swept out Peterson's store. Miss Harper gave me a nickel, and Mr. Peterson gave me a dime. I worked with Pa on the oyster beds and with Ma and Gran'ma picking beach plums and making jelly and jam. There was no money in working for your family, though.

But there were ways. It used to be in September that tinker blues came into Smalltown harbor. Even when we were seven or eight, Frank and I used to fish off the wharves for them whenever the tides were right. We had long bamboo poles with spreaders on the lines, and we hopped like mad when the little fish were hitting. Mr. Beers at the fish market paid us 25 cents a bushel for them. Some days Frank and I made a couple of dollars. We don't have those fish anymore, sad to say.

Some days we could catch them so fast that we would take turns dragging them to the market. Soon as we filled a basket, one of us would haul a wagon up to Mr. Beers's place. About a mile it was, so it would take some time. The one left fishing would work like crazy, tending maybe eight, ten poles.

One time, walking the flats on an extreme neap tide, Frank and I, we were about nine maybe, came on an old oyster bed. It wasn't marked or anything, and it was obvious that nobody had been working on it for a long time.

Robert Wolley

We didn't tell anyone, but when we had such low tides, we started taking care of the bed. We did a lot of work, repiling the rocks and shells and dragging a slew of new stuff to the bed. Oysters have to have something to grab hold of, old shells and rocks or bricks or whatever, or else they grab each other and smother each other, or when they're real small they get carried off by the tides. We completely rebuilt the bed, using the knowledge gained from watching the oystermen and my work with my pa. We went up Big Swamp river to find new oysters and transplanted them. That was hard work because there were few oysters or beds that did not belong to someone else.

All summer we worked and way into the fall. Some days in the winter, even, we went to check the bed, and by the next spring it was doing very well. Winter is a particularly hard time for shallow water oystermen. If there is a lot of ice that moves in and out with the tides, the beds can be dragged all over and even lost completely, the oysters going wherever their holding stones go.

Now, every single person that went to the harbor knew that we were working that old bed. We got lots of advice, and, of course, being way out on the flats where it never gets completely uncovered, we had to work fast. All the men watched out for us. Somebody gave us long poles we were to carry always in case we stumbled into deep, endless muck or quicksand. We were to use the poles to support ourselves because usually the poles would reach clear across the bad holes. And we were never to walk too close together, so if one went in, the other would be there to help or to get help.

That summer we decided to harvest a few oysters and sell them to Mr. Beers. Old man Prince, who had more beds than anyone and knew everything there was to know about oysters, came out to tell us how many to take and which ones and how to keep a proper bed.

The Pranks An' Enlightenment of Frank An' Me

We didn't ask Mr. Prince; he just came one day. "Sees ya youn'sters workin' hard," he said. "Maybe ya take an ol' hand's help a mite." We knew he must have checked out the bed and figured that we were doing okay, or at least trying to, otherwise he would not have bothered with us. That was the way folks were; hard work brought the reward of others helping.

Oysters once had been prime for living, but years back something happened, disease or something, and for a long time there were no oysters. Then, when Pa was a young man, all the oystermen got together and had thousands of seed oysters shipped to Smalltown from Maryland. Those were the seeds of the Smalltown oysters we have now. By the time Frank and I had got in the business, the oyster harvest had been abundant for years.

Now the good and bad part. Frank and I took just two bushels of oysters on Mr. Prince's wisdom, and he knowing so much, we stuck to that number. We dragged our wagon all the way to Mr. Beers' place, two miles or more. He gave us a dollar a bushel, saying that he could not pay more because he didn't know the quality. He said that was a fair price. We knew that it wasn't.

Frank and I had a little conversation and decided to say nothing, figuring we would find some other place to sell the oysters next time. Of course, we knew that there was no other place.

As we were leaving, Mr. Beers said, "Now, boys, I knows ya both think I'm acheatin' ya. But business is business, an' even little ones should know that."

Then Mr. Beers did a surprising thing. "Now, I wants ta give ya each 'nother dollar," he said, "but not for them oysters, 'cause ya knows I got ta tend ta business."

"Why then?" asked Frank.

"'Cause I wants ya business. Now two dollars more'n fair, but I gives but one dollar for the oysters."

I didn't understand. "Then why are you giving us more?"

"Gentlemen's agreement," Mr. Beers said. "I knows you'll go ta Peterson's an' buy some cheap candy, but I's trustin' you'll save some of that extra dollar an' maybe buy a few seeds from Prince so later you'll bring me more o' ya oysters."

Now, that was something.

The next summer, between all the other things going on, Frank and I had a big harvest, so big that Mr. Prince hauled for us in his wagon.

And by then the price of oysters had shot way up, and Mr. Beers paid us what he paid the others, three dollars, seventy-five cents a bushel. We were rich! In August we made out last delivery to Mr. Beers, just like every other oysterman, and some of the oystermen praised us for our hard work.

That night, sitting at home with Ma and Gran'ma, Pa was long gone by then, a state trooper came to the house, and believe me, when one of them came to your house, something was mighty wrong.

Smalltown never did have a policeman, always relying on the state police if law enforcement was needed. First, we thought it was Pa in some kind of trouble.

But it was me — and Frank.

Right off the man said that we owed some man in Pilot over a hundred dollars for taking his oysters. Then he said Ma could be arrested for allowing her child to engage in criminal activity. And then he said there would be a fine on top of it all.

Well, Ma threw a fit. The trooper finally saw that it was no use talking about it that night and told Ma that he would see all of us in court.

We rushed up to Frank's house. The same thing had happened there. We were in a heap of trouble.

A lot of papers came to the house, official papers, and finally we all had to go to Barnstable and appear before some judge. Even Mr. Beers went, and Mr. Prince. Mr. Beers had to go

The Pranks An' Enlightenment of Frank An' Me

because he was charged with buying stolen goods. Mr. Prince wanted to go because he wanted to testify for all of us. Mr. Prince didn't have to go, but Gran'ma said he was going to speak on our behalf and for some of the other oystermen from Smalltown in our favor.

In the end, Frank and I lost the oyster bed and all the money we got from Mr. Beers. The judge gave us back the little we had spent on seed oysters, one dollar, eighty cents. He said he was sorry that the seventy-five dollars we had earned had to go to the man who owned the bed. At least he didn't fine Ma or Frank's folks, but he did take a sizable amount from Mr. Beers, a hundred dollars, so Mr. Beers lost most of all.

In spite of that, I think Mr. Prince was the most upset. He said something to the judge and got fined five dollars. When Mr. Prince paid that, he asked the judge how much to say something more. The judge said ten dollars. Mr. Prince opened his money purse and told the judge that he had twenty more dollars and wanted to have a say about hard-working boys and let-go beds and how Smalltown people were honest and God-fearing and all the rest. The judge said he had heard it all before. Mr. Prince said no he had not, so the judge took ten of Mr. Prince's dollars and told him that if he had anything more to say he would go to jail.

That was the end of Frank and me in a real business until just before the war when we went in partnership with our own fishing boat.

When Mr. Beers and Mr. Prince got back to Smalltown, they spread the word about what happened, and I think because of that Frank and I got to working some on the fishing and scallop boats. We weren't much as hands go, but we cut bait and sorted fish and kept the boats clean and made coffee and sandwiches and such. There was little pay, never was, but it helped out at home.

I don't know where Frank's parents got the money to pay up; Gran'ma took our share out of her burying fund, she said. "Jest make my box a mite smaller," she said. Of course, all the

Robert Wolley

money I made had gone to necessary things, to pay some family bills but mostly for clothes and such which I wouldn't have had. Funny thing, that bed never was touched again. I am not going to tell you the man's name; vowed I'd never speak it and I won't, but he sent word through his lawyer that he would sell Frank and me the bed for nine hundred dollars. Doesn't that beat all.

The Pranks An' Enlightenment of Frank An' Me

Chapter II

Some Of The Captains An' Their Boats

Robert Wolley

During the 1938 hurricane with no name, I was working a quarter share on Benny Costa's dragger, the *S, M and J*. They were the initials of his gran'children, although I always figured they were for his special, and his only, way of swearing.

Benny never spoke dirty words, the four letter kind you hear today; he always said the same thing, "Sweet Mary an' Joseph." The way he said it mattered, though. He could say it as sweet as pie or as mean and hard as any cruel human being could. It depended on the situation, like the hurricane. Besides the wind and water noises, that is what I remember hearing the most, "Sweet Mary an' Joseph."

As I say, I was on Benny's boat, and we were well southeast of the islands, twenty, thirty miles maybe. We knew a storm had come up, a real bad one, and rather suddenly, too. What forecasts there were had suggested that a bad storm would be well south and west of New England, with no threat to us.

Lordy, did it blow. Maybe no more than other bad storms, but Benny said it was worse, and after a while it blew harder than anything I had ever imagined. Being Cap'n, Benny elected to take us more to the east.

That didn't set too well with the others, but it was a good thing he did. Anyway, we were pounding like 'ell, and all the while Benny was saying "Sweet Mary an' Joseph." First it was an expression of astonishment, then it was downright anger and hate, and at the last it was more a prayer then anything else.

Wind and waves. Lord A'mighty there were waves. When we were on top of a particularly big one, we could see coming toward us a monster wave, fifty, sixty feet high. Never in my worst nightmares was there a wave that huge bearing down on me.

Benny headed right into it, bow first. We careened down the backside of one wave smack into the middle of the monster. At first the bow lifted, and for an instant I thought we were going to be fine, but as the bow lifted, it was obvious that the boat was

The Pranks An' Enlightenment of Frank An' Me

going to stand on its end and be somersaulted backward. Benny gave the old boat every ounce of power it had, all the time yelling, "Go, go. Sweet Mary an' Joseph, go!"

The wave started to break and broke right over us. That undoubtedly saved our boat and our lives. As it was, the wave carried most everything away, and would have carried us away, too, if Benny hadn't made us tie ourselves to the boat. Part of the wheelhouse went, along with most of the dragging equipment and the stack and dory. Everything except a part of the mast went, and that broke about three feet over our heads. The four of us, Benny, Tom Crocker, Bill Yule, and I, were tied to that mast, and except for a lot of bruises and Tom's broken finger, we were uninjured.

I had been terrified, and when it was all over, I found that I had messed my pants, not just wet them, but messed them for good.

After that wave, it was just a storm, bad but no worse than some nor'easters. Our greatest danger was the lack of steering, and we were at the mercy of the waves for hours as the men tried to rig up a steering device, which they finally were able to do with a hatch cover. At first we all took turns with the manual pumps. Benny had flooded the fish hold trying to make the boat ride easier. But with the big wave, we had taken in far more water than was safe, and with each wave we took in hundreds of gallons, and once the hatch cover was removed for our steering, water came in in tons. While the men worked, I was left to do the pumping. Several times I would have quit if it hadn't been so obvious that my life depended on it.

We never lost the engine. That was the second miracle, the first being that we were alive.

To this day I don't know how we kept going or how in the wind and rain and pitch dark the men could do what they had to do, and through it all hardly a word was spoken and never more than a two word sentence. "Take this," "hold on," "watch out,"

Robert Wolley

"over there" were enough. I guess there are no speeches required when it comes to life and death. One strange recollection I have is that I never did think about dying; as scared as I was, I never thought I was going to die.

We were going to Providence, if Benny could find it, that is, navigation being by dead reckoning, but after a day and a half, we met other boats and found out that that port was completely gone. So were most of the other alternative ports. From other boats we borrowed materials and food and a compass, and with some help from other crews our steering was improved. Benny elected to go to Provincetown, as did five other boats, and we sailed as a convoy to that place. I didn't want to leave the S,M and J, but Benny made me call Ma and go home.

As I have told the story, I have made the wave grow. The fact is, I don't know how high it was. I tell you fifty or sixty feet and could tell you one hundred feet; that's what I have told some people. The truth is, maybe, that the wave was as high as I say, but I know I kept adding to it once until it got to one hundred feet. It was as high as the top of the Methodist church steeple, truthfully. And it sounded like an express train.

And I will tell you something else, too. Hardly a fisherman can swim worth a lick. Oh, we all learn when we are young, but no fisherman I ever knew went in the water unless it was an emergency. Some day look at the fishermen. They are as white as ghosts above their arms and below their necks. They never take their shirts and pants off, and *never* go near the beach, and *never* go swimming. And that is the truth, too.

Mostly they were small fishing boats, the boats I worked on as a boy. Two or three men, or two men and a boy, or three men and a boy, that size crew, except for the few times I worked on the schooners. Then there were eight or ten men — and maybe two boys, if two boys were available, which wasn't always, there being a scarcity of boys my age.

The Pranks An' Enlightenment of Frank An' Me

And mostly we did the same things as the men but in lesser amounts, and seldom did we do the dangerous work unless there was an emergency. Sometimes it seemed that we did only those things that kept the men going, making coffee and sandwiches, lots of both when the fishing was good for long stretches. And the few times I sailed with Cap'n Hines, keeping his cigars lit.

Lord A'mighty, how I hated that. Cap'n Hines had a cigar in his mouth from the day he was weaned, so his crew said, and I think it was true. But when the work got going, Cap'n Hines would forget to suck on the cigar, and it would go out. Then he'd hand it to me. "Light this, boy," he'd yell, and I had to, and it was disgusting because the mouth end would be all chewed and wet. I'd keep my eye on Cap'n Hines' cigar, sometimes when I ought to have been tending to something else, and when I'd see that no smoke was coming forth, I'd try to find myself busy elsewhere. Wasn't any use though. He'd find me and shove the thing into my hand. "Light this, boy."

I guess he did the same to all the boys, and he being captain meant there wasn't much you could do but obey. I never did take up the cigar, though, and just thinking about it gets my stomach rolling.

The captains always had little habits that were peculiar and, I think, unique to them.

Cap'n Moniz could be standing in a rain coming down heavier than The Flood and always he would hold out his hand and say, "I guess it's rainin' a mite" or "I think it's rainin' pretty good." It wasn't his saying but his saying with his hand reaching out that tickled me so, as though he didn't know it was raining until he reached out and felt it.

I was working on his dragger one day when the winch skipped because of a couple of cogs missing from the main gear. The drag line got wrapped on the rudder, which was unusual because all fishing boats have some kind of skeg to prevent that sort of thing from happening. But it happens and usually can be cleared from the deck. That day it couldn't be, and Cap'n Moniz decided finally to use the dory carried on the pilot house. With the net out and the winch holding everything, that meant hard work.

As the dory was being unleashed, it began to rain. Out went the captain's hand. "I guess it's rainin' a mite." A bit more than a mite, I thought.

The dory was launched finally and the captain wanted me to row. By then it was raining about as hard as it possibly could. I put the captain stern to, and while Sam and Irwin worked from above, Cap'n Moniz worked with his head and arms in the water, coming up now and then for a breath.

The dory must have leaked a bit; it never rained any harder; we were collecting water at an alarming rate. I though about bailing but two oars were needed to hold the dory steady and in position.

First there was a few inches of water, then there was a foot, and then the water was almost to the thwart, so maybe there was a good twelve or thirteen inches. I waited for the captain to come up for air and pointed to the water.

I don't think he comprehended my meaning for a minute or so. He looked at the water, then stuck out his hand. "Boy," he asked, "don't you know it's rainin'?"

Now, one of the wonders of the dory is the load it can carry, but the load has to be more or less stable, not like the water that sloshes from side to side with the slightest movement, always seeking its own level, and when there's enough moving water, threatening to capsize the dory.

"When water comes in, boy," the captain said, "body has to bail."

The Pranks An' Enlightenment of Frank An' Me

"I'm suggestin' we take a minute so that be done," I answered. "Can't hold ya where ya wants to be and bail at the same time."

"Boy, I'm cap'n 'cause I already figured that out. When the water come in the top of my boats, I had a sense that ya wasn't bailin'. That an' the enlightenin' fact that either my arms was gettin' longer or the dory here was settlin' some."

With that said he got to laughing. "Bail, son! Cap'n's orders."

Then he got serious because he called me son. When the captains wanted to get something across, sooner or later they addressed you as son.

"Son," Cap'n Moniz said, "no matter what, you've got to take care of your boat. Lose the boat, you're lost. Today we're never in danger, but this here dory still your boat, an' it needed tendin' to. I got concentratin' on other things, so ya had to stay alert. Take charge, son, an' explain later if ya have to."

Which was by way of saying that I was delinquent in my bailing, but he never said that, never attached anything mean or sinister or remotely of direct blame to it, but I got the lesson, one that would be reinforced over and over again by all of the captains: take care of the boat so it can take care of you.

Cap'n Max had one of the nicest boats to work on because he took care of his crew with a special affection. Seldom did he take a boy on board, but when he did you knew that he was planning to fish until he filled every inch of space, and sometimes that meant several days of hard work.

Cap'n Max had a reputation of sorts. If the fish were deep, he would be fishing in the shallows; if the fish were in the shallows, he would be fishing deep. Sooner or later he'd get it right, and always he was one of the profitable fishermen, although fishing with him could mean long days. I fished with him a number of times.

Robert Wolley

Once, after three days, we had so few fish you could count them. "How many we got?" he asked once, meaning to get an estimate in pounds.

Jimmy Lane shouted, "twenty-four," which the captain took to mean twenty-four hundred pounds.

"Can't be," said Cap'n Max. "We ain't anywhere near that weight."

"No," says Jimmy. "I mean we got twenty-four fish. I figured that our by countin' them eyes an' dividin' by two. Give me somethin' to do with my schoolin'."

Of course, Jimmy was exaggerating some, but not overly much, and for once Cap'n Max returned home with little to show for the three days.

When he thanked me for crewing, he gave me the nine dollars we had agreed on and fifty cents to have some fun. I knew we hadn't caught enough fish to pay for the gas and said so, telling him that maybe he'd like to pay me later. No, he said, the crew would get nothing because they worked on shares, but when he took on someone for wages, he paid. That way he knew I'd work again.

"Besides," he said, "none of my crew is starvin' 'cause there's always them twenty-four fish. Ought to last a couple of days." And as he was saying that, he took a couple of fish and said they were for Ma and Gran'ma. And would I take a few more for various widows who lived along my way home.

Cap'n Max always sent fish to the widows no matter what. When I asked him once why he never failed to do that, he said that when he was a boy and his father drowned, every fisherman always sent a fish to his mother. "Kept us from starvin', I think, an' I honor those who saved us by doin' the same."

I worked just once for Cap'n L _ _ _ . Actually, Frank and I did. For some reason that I don't remember, Gran'ma was displeased with the prospect of my working for the man, but she

The Pranks An' Enlightenment of Frank An' Me

didn't press it and I didn't give it much regard at the time. The captain wasn't from Smalltown, but he'd haul in once in a while looking for a crew. As far as I knew, he had a profitable boat.

Anyway, he came in one summer day; Frank and I took his lines and helped him tie up. He thanked us and said we could help ourselves to a fish each for our efforts. He was going to unload his catch, already had made the arrangements, and if we wanted to work in the hold, he'd be much obliged.

Working in the hold was nothing much, smelly though, and if you didn't have proper boots painful because of all the fins ready to stick you. So we said yes, figuring that boots could be borrowed, so we hung around for a while waiting for the fish truck and wondering where the captain's crew was.

(We didn't know at the time that the Cap'n had been struck a little peculiar and that his crew had demanded to be put ashore.)

But the prospect of making a little money took our attention to other thoughts, and Cap'n L _ _ _ soon returned with truck and driver. We asked for boots, and the captain said he had some but we'd have to rent them.

"How much?" Frank asked.

"Fifty cents each," the captain said.

"And how much are we going to be paid?" Frank asked again.

Two dollars was the answer.

"That's not much for all the work," I remember saying, "'specially if ya takin' fifty cents away for a pair o' boots."

"Boy, ya got your 'rithmetic wrong. Boots is fifty cents each, a dollar a pair."

"Then we hope ya enjoy you'self," shouted Frank, and we walked away.

"Wait a minute!"

"Five dollars each," yelled Frank, "and no charge for the boots."

"That's robbery. That's ten dollars. That's more than a man'd get."

"But I don't see no men," and I pointed around the wharf. "No men nowhere."

We settled on three dollars each, and no rent on the boots.

Frank and I went into the hold and started pitching fish into the basket. When the first basket got to the deck, the Cap'n started yelling again.

"You're spoilin' my catch. Look at all them pitchfork holes." And he started swearing at us. Then he yelled down, "I want them fish in the basket by hand; no marks; every fish just as clean an' whole as the way God made 'em."

Later we would find out that Cap'n L _ _ _ was supplying a company that advertised its fish as "natural," and that no blemishes were allowed, even to having an open gill where one might grab a fish. We had to pick up each fish by the tail and carefully place it in the basket.

Once we got our learning from Cap'n L _ _ _ it all went well, and when he paid us off, he gave us the first basket of fish and said he hoped we could sell it, which of course we could and did right away.

Then he asked us if we wanted to crew for him the next couple of days. We settled on a price, which was fair according to what we had been earning, but when I asked him why he would want two boys when there were men who were looking for work, he said that two boys were better and cheaper.

When I went home that night and told Ma that I had a berth for a couple of days, she was not as delighted as I thought she would be, but she didn't say anything. It was Gran'ma who objected some, but she didn't press the matter, just said to Ma that sometimes a boy needed a father. I had no idea what that was all about, except that Gran'ma was forever saying that.

The Pranks An' Enlightenment of Frank An' Me

The next morning I met Frank and he said that his ma and pa didn't take to the idea of his going, and if I wasn't going, he couldn't, but he didn't know why his folks felt that way.

We went out with Cap'n L _ _ _ and he was nice enough. His boat was real clean and every piece of equipment and machinery was spotless even if some of it was old and well used.

We were a little mystified when Cap'n L _ _ _ told us that he fished only on sunny days, but that mystery got cleared up fast. When we got to where the captain said we were going to drop the trawl, he started taking off his clothes. "Come on, boys. Off with everything. This here boat fishes *au natural*," or something like that.

I looked at Frank and he looked back at me. By now Cap'n L _ _ _ was stark naked. "Hurry up, boys. Off with them clothes. The fish is waitin'."

Well, maybe they were, but I'd never in my whole life fished naked. I'd never ever fished without a shirt on, and I wasn't about to take everything off. I guess Frank felt the same way because he just stood there, looking dumb.

"Now, boys. This is nature's own way. We was born naked and we'll meet our Creator naked. Clothes ain't natural, ain't God's way."

Now, I have to jump ahead and tell you that Cap'n L _ _ _, I found out later, was what some folks called a "naturist;" nudists we called them. The captain never was more than that, never even was talked about as doing more than enjoying the sun. Freedom, he called it.

But at the time, Frank and I called it downright queer, and we refused. I did tell the captain that I'd take off my shirt but nothing more. He gave in finally, and nothing more was said about the strange naked captain and his boy crew.

Until I got home, that is, and then both Ma and Gran'ma pestered me about the trip. Nothing happened, I told them, although finally I got around to telling them about seeing the cap'n bare.

"Lord, he's a strange one," offered Gran'ma.

"You didn't take off your clothes?" Ma became obsessed with knowing that. I hadn't, but denying it didn't seem to count for much because there always was a little bit of suspicion lingering in Ma's eyes.

Funny thing, Gran'ma and Cap'n L _ _ _ became close friends later on. I never went on his boat again, and after the war started up, I never saw or heard about him either. But when Gran'ma died, he came to the service. Said he always inquired about us and was right sorry about Gran'ma. He even came to the house for a few minutes after the service. He had given up fishing, he said, but he hadn't given up "the freedom of the sun" as he put it.

Frank and I got to know almost all of the captains, if not face to face then by reputation. There were few bad captains, but there were a few, none from Smalltown as far as I know. I don't think a bad captain would have been able to live in our town, small as it was and where everybody was so connected to everyone else and all so dependent on each other in so many ways.

In the bigger fish ports there were tales of miserable captains, some even brutal. Frank and I were both working for Cap'n Lyle once. I don't remember how we both got to be on his boat at the same tie, but anyway, we pulled into Vineyard Haven on Martha's Vineyard to avoid a storm, and because Cap'n Lyle didn't have too much knowledge about the waters we were trying to fish.

For some reason that I don't remember, if I ever knew, he had decided to try his hand at swordfishing, having heard that eastward of Nantucket and Martha's Vineyard a fortune was to

The Pranks An' Enlightenment of Frank An' Me

be had. Swordfishing was new to me and Frank, so we were on an adventure. Besides, we had never been to the islands.

Cap'n Lyle seemed to know what he was about, though, although he kept an eye on his charts, particularly once we got south of Chatham, and he made sure that every crew member, Frank and I included, got to feel the currents by taking the wheel. We were, he said, in some of the most dangerous waters around the Cape. But in truth, I don't remember it being bad at all. Later, when I was older and responsible for a ship, I would regret having entered the area, but on this day everything was calm and quiet.

We passed between Nantucket and the Cape at night, picking up the lights from Great Point on Nantucket and Monomoy and Stage Harbor in Chatham. The plan was to sail between Nantucket and Martha's Vineyard and to fish off the south side of the Vineyard and down toward Block Island, but by the time we picked up the Nantucket Harbor light, Brant lighthouse, we were buffeted by strong northwest winds. Cap'n Lyle said he thought it best to take shelter on Martha's Vineyard, so we picked up the lights at Cape Poge and the Chops and headed toward Vineyard Haven where Cap'n Lyle said we would take on fuel and wait out the wind. We tied up at about 5:30 that morning.

We weren't greeted too kindly by one particular fishing boat and there was some to-do about Cap'n Lyle tying up and taking the place of a Vineyard Haven boat that was overdue. I don't remember any of the details, just one, and that was bad enough.

Cap'n Lyle, to avoid any argument, decided to seek an anchorage. He put me and Frank off, gave us each a dollar, and told us we could walk to the center of town. And if we could hitch a ride, we might be able to get to Edgartown. He pointed out the way.

And he was very specific about our returning to the wharf no later than four o'clock. Someone would row us out to the boat, but he was going to let the men have some time ashore that night, and Frank and I would be on watch.

Since it was so early, Frank and I looked forward to a full day exploring a new town. We hadn't gone far when a lad about our age caught up. Frank and I were thirteen, as I remember.

"Ya cap'n gave ya money," the boy said. We must have looked at him suspiciously. "Oh, I ain't gonna rob ya. Not that I could take on the likes of you two. Jest seems a mighty fine thing ya cap'n done."

"Well, he's a good man," Frank replied. "He knows we ain't got no cash an' that we got hopes for a tonic an' stuff."

"More than 'nough, I would say."

"You workin' for that sour cap'n we tied up next to? He weren't none too friendly. We're only here 'cause the weather's so bad." I wanted to say that the greeting we got was worse than the weather, but I let it go at that.

"Ya. I made a few trips with him. My pa owes him money an' I'm helpin' pay it off."

"Why ain't ya pa workin'?" I asked.

"Got a broken leg. Works for Cap'n Baggs, he do, but can't do much now. While back the captain give him some money to see us through a mite, but now the captain wants his money back."

"That was Cap'n Baggs, I suppose." Frank turned up his nose.

"That were 'im."

"Money's tight," I offered. "Maybe he's havin' trouble, too."

"Maybe; maybe not. But he owns three boats, 'though he can't get crews for 'em. Cruel man."

"How so?" I wanted to know.

"You're cap'n ever strike ya?"

"Lord, no. He wouldn't dare. Don't think the thought ever came to him."

"You's lucky." The boy lifted the back of his sweater. "Look. This is Baggs's way of learnin' me."

The Pranks An' Enlightenment of Frank An' Me

I had never seen lash marks, but I suppose what I saw would be them. And some were fresh, still bleeding.

"What the hell did you do?"

"I spilled some of the captain's coffee."

"That's all?"

"That were 'nough."

The boy walked away. I felt sick and angry.

"That certainly spoils a good day," Frank said. "Can't believe that the people here would allow such a thing."

Frank and I walked around a bit, then hiked over to Oak Bluffs where once I had relatives, so I was told. And we managed to ride to Edgartown where we spent our dollar. But what was supposed to be a fun day was not. The sight of that boy's back took away any pleasure we might have had.

Cap'n Lyle was surprised to see us so solemn. He asked us if we had found trouble, and in turn we asked him if he would beat us if we had.

"Of course not. What ya do that prompts such a question?"

And we told him about the boy and Baggs and the boy's father and all.

"Boys, I ain't never struck another person in my whole life. I've wanted to a few times, I admit, but I never did. Come to think on it, I don't know of a single boat owner that has ever laid a hand on man or boy. Until now, I ain't never even heard of such a thing as striking a boy."

I don't know whether the captain had planned to go ashore that night, but he did not. While Frank and I had the watch, as it were, Cap'n Lyle stayed on board. I had the feeling that he was protecting us, but from what I have no idea. Perhaps he was simply showing us that he cared for and about us, something that we already sensed and knew.

None of the captains had children the age of Frank and me. Our particular age made us unique, although that insight came to me much later in life. Always, we were treated by the captains as

Robert Wolley

they would have treated their own sons, or in a couple of instances, as younger brothers. Frank and I were part of an extended family. I didn't know that phrase at the time, and I certainly didn't think of myself as a member of so many families. Again, it was one of those insights that came later, but it was true even if we didn't realize it at the time.

This enlightenment came to me only after Frank died in the war. I was working out some arrangement or other with Mr. Beers and said something to the effect that I wished Frank could be there to take care of business matters, he having been so good at that.

Mr. Beers said something I have never forgotten. I quote him, although I'm probably putting words into his mouth. But he said something like this: "Son, Frank's ma and pa suffered a great loss, and you suffered a great loss. To lose a son is a terrible thing; to lose your best friend is just about as terrible. I can't think of anything that could be much worse for either Frank's parents or for you. But believe me, son, when I tell you that the whole town still cries for the loss of its child." The tears on his cheeks testified to his feelings.

And then he added one more thought. "We think of all the children as our children. I mean mine. You and Frank are my children, or Frank was and you still are. You are the promise of what our lives are all about."

There was a little bit more that I remember, but you catch the drift of what Mr. Beers was expressing. Needless to say, we shed a few tears that day and ended up hugging each other. I especially remember that because I had never hugged a man before, not even Frank.

And I remember that after that day with Mr. Beers, every now and then one or another of the captains would put an arm on my shoulder, and I realized that with that gesture they were expressing both love and support. I never have forgotten how absolutely meaningful such touching could be and how

The Pranks An' Enlightenment of Frank An' Me

important it was both then and now. The few times I have recalled such occasions, I have been questioned about "manliness" or asked whether I didn't find such affection troubling or even immoral. I resent the negative suggestions and decide them unworthy of any comment.

Most of the captains named their boats, but if you looked carefully it was obvious that the name was almost an afterthought, hastily painted to do honor to one's wife or children or to a historical or mythical character. Sometimes the reality was that the one so honored did the lettering, usually in a less than professional way. Yachts have professional gold leaf lettering; fishing boats use borrowed paint and unsteady hands.

For a time Harper Melvin fished out of our harbor: five or six years as I remember. I never was on his boat, but it was a joy to behold because of the topside paint job. Harper was in his thirties, was a free spirit, and had, so I was led to believe, a girl in every port.

His boat's topside colors were a rainbow — or a garishly offensive display — of every leftover can of paint he could find that had a few brushfulls of paint. It didn't matter the color. Black led into red and white into blue and green into purple and brown into yellow. Some of the brushstrokes were horizontal, some were vertical: whatever was needed to fill in the spaces was done and used. And there were plenty of runs caused by the failure to brush out the paint. An uglier mess never existed.

Except for a rectangle on each bow side. There in a perfectly formed space was the name of his boat. Betty. Or Dora. Or Janice. Or Anna. Or Shirley. Or Wilma. The girl of the moment had her name emblazoned on Harper's bow. The trouble was, sometimes he was too busy changing names to fish. Emma, Gladys, Patience, Charity, Freddie, Marion; I have left out dozens of names.

Robert Wolley

I heard someone suggest once that the boat be named "Girl" or "Female" and be done with it, but it never worked out, I guess. It was suggested also that the boat be outfitted with interchangeable boards, that way a lot of paint would be saved.

One story about Harper involves his taking his current (if temporary) girlfriend along on a fishing trip. He is alleged to have picked up a girl by the name of Agnes and, as the *Agnes* was making its way to the fishing grounds, to have proudly showed Agnes her name on the bow. For some reason or other, Agnes had to rub her hand on the name, and Harper had to hold her over the side so she could do that.

The paint was still fresh, and as Agnes swept her hand over her own name, another name appeared. Agnes had Harper haul her up, slapped his face, and demanded to be taken home immediately. If he failed to do so, she would file charges against him, kidnapping or alienation of affection or some such thing.

Naturally, Harper had to accommodate Agnes. Never one to miss a beat, Harper had an alternative plan. Since Agnes was no longer the girl of the moment, Harper got out his paint and brush, washed the remains of Agnes's name off both sides of the bow, and prepared to letter on a new girlfriend's name.

This got Agnes upset, to say the least. As Harper was doing his painting, Agnes gave him an assist, and he fell into the water, paint and all.

Harper's crew at that time was Jeffery Gay. Jeffery was from parts unknown; at least everyone wondered where he came from. He was in and out of Smalltown now and then. Never stayed long if he wasn't hired on. Jeffery was one huge fellow, six feet six or eight, at least three hundred pounds, and an absolutely tireless worker. But he was dumber than a dead cod. He could hardly walk without being told which foot to move. Give him a specific job and it would be done to perfection; give him two jobs, he would do the first and completely forget the second; ask him to do innovate or to use his initiative, he was hopelessly lost.

The Pranks An' Enlightenment of Frank An' Me

So when Harper fell overboard, or was pushed, Jeffery was at a total loss. At the moment of Harper's swim, Jeffery was steering a westerly course. And that is what he continued to do. When it became apparent to Agnes that Jeffery was not going to save Harper and that she probably would be accused of murder, she had to give him directions.

Regretfully, Agnes was not familiar with either boats or the role of command, so it was some time before she got Jeffery's undivided attention and dubious cooperation. What transpired from the time of Harper's unplanned dive to his rescue is unknown. I can only guess that Agnes more than earned her brief moment as a name on a fishing boat's bow.

Now, those in the know claimed that a ruffled and I-suddenly-got-religion Harper gracefully deposited Agnes on the appropriate wharf and left quickly for other parts. But it seems that the I-got-religion part didn't last long. Sometimes, having cheated death, men get a sense of invulnerability. Harper steered a course toward another girl, one named Laura.

And while Jeffery steered the designated course, Harper leaned over the bow and painted a new name. As the story goes, Harper did find Laura, and she agreed to sail with him. But that romance floundered when Laura spied her name on Harper's boat.

He had printed it upside down.

And then there was Essy Rose, captain of the *Saint With No Name*, originally a 38-foot trawler built, I always thought, with wood from the Ark. The Saint With No Name had more cracks in her sides and stern than there are stars in the sky. She leaked at a frightful rate, and on her mooring she looked as I imagined a fireboat looked, her pumps spouting water from a dozen places and always with some force.

Robert Wolley

Every plank looked like the end of an unwhipped rope, frayed and tattered. And every plank had scores of nail and screw holes where the captain had tried to refasten his ancient hull. One thing about Cap'n Rose was that no matter where he tied his dory, the Saint With No Name always filled it with bilge water so that the dory was always half sunk and Cap'n Rose was forever pumping it out.

With a boat like that, one became either a raving tartar or a humorous philosopher. Cap'n Rose was the latter. He had a secure and fundamental belief in fate, so what was the use of fighting against rot and rust? The name of his boat testified to his belief because somewhere there was a saint watching over him. He didn't know which saint it was, so, like addressing prayers to an unknown God, he named his boat for that unknown saint in whose hands he was.

"I got two wives," he said to me one day. "They're both a bit frayed an' unsightly, an' they both leak a bit, I fear, but they're long lastin' an' faithful an' I love 'em both."

Essy was in his sixties; Alva, Cap'n Rose used to say, "was a good fifteen years older. An' when I say good, boy, I mean good, 'cause I was jest like you be, young an' stupid, an' she teached me everythin'."

Alva, according to Gran'ma, had been Essy's ninth grade teacher. When Essy decided to quit school, Alva offered to teach him at night. They ended up getting married, which lost Alva her teaching job, at least in the schoolhouse, and forced Essy to work even harder. Already he was supporting his mother and father. They died before I was born.

Alva worked alongside Essy. She had to give that up when I was small, but I do have one memory of watching the pair unload their catch. Every step of the way Alva was teaching Essy. Later, I supposed that she was teaching much as Socrates is said to have taught, and I must say that while his language was

The Pranks An' Enlightenment of Frank An' Me

unrefined, Cap'n Rose possessed encyclopedic knowledge about the world and about history. He recited the poets and Greek dramatists, revealed the scriptures of countless religions, told about people in faraway places, and unfolded their customs. He knew the major philosophers by name and recounted their theories.

Alva was a wonderful old woman. Her sense of humor was as large as she was, and she was expansive. She and Essy were two loving, good-natured souls, different from any others I knew up to that time. Although I never worked on the Saint With No Name, whenever the opportunity came around to listen in on him, I did, and always with rapt attention.

Que sera, sera was Cap'n Rose's motto. Nothing could upset him. He was given to quoting certain Latin phrases. One he used frequently was *credo quia adsurdum est,* I believe because it is absurd. And he seemed bent on proving both his belief and life's absurdities. The Saint With No Name was one of those absurdities.

Cap'n Rose and Alva tended fish weirs. They had set hundreds of poles or stakes parallel to the shore, strung miles of nets, and set the huge circular net at the end of the passageway. It was a gigantic undertaking for one man and one woman. How they managed to haul the capture nets by themselves and with that boat is beyond me. But they did. And when Alva had to give up, Cap'n Rose did all of the work by himself. By itself, the seamanship alone impressed me because every other weirman was using small boats and lots of manpower.

In early spring cod and haddock found the weirs; shortly thereafter the flounder started moving, then the mackerel and stripers came, and then the bluefish. Cap'n Rose said he had studied the Indian methods and that with fate's kindness and his patience, all the fish he could want would come to him.

But two other fish also came, dogfish or sand sharks and horse mackerel, school tuna of one hundred fifty to two hundred pounds. The sharks were bad enough because they could chase everything out of the enclosure; the tuna were big enough to tear up the nets. At that time horse mackerel were not a commercial fish.

One day Cap'n Rose found his nets destroyed totally. The tuna had struck again. He gave up the weir, spending weeks taking up the stakes. Someone asked him what he was going to do.

"Fate has given me a golden opportunity. I'm goin' to go catch horse mackerel."

Folks thought he had lost his mind. As it turned out, Cap'n Rose was ahead of his time. First, he rerigged his trawler in what he said was the fashion of the Pacific Ocean tuna catchers; then he set to building the lures, gigantic silver spoons with huge hooks, and strange-looking bamboo poles wrapped every few inches with tarred linen line to keep the pole from cracking; and finally, he attached a heavy line to the end of each pole, twelve or fifteen feet long, each line about three feet shorter than the pole.

In the center of the Saint With No Name he erected a tower which he would climb and from which he hoped to spot the fish. Horse mackerel are a school fish, and once sighted and held together as a school with generous amounts of chum, Cap'n Rose figured he could catch a boat load.

He did well except for one thing I'll mention in a moment, so well, in fact, that a few years after his initial success, a whole new industry started up: sportfishing for school tuna. And not too many years later, when the true value of the school tuna was realized, the heavy commercial and sport fishing pressure reduced the tuna population to almost nothing.

But at the time, Cap'n Rose failed to acknowledge that there was no market for his fish. An occasional bluefin tuna might be brought in, and there was a food market for that fish, but the only market for horse mackerel was as fertilizer, and no one was buying.

"*Audentes fortuna juvat*," he would say. "*Dum spiro, spero.*" Fortune favors the bold; while I breathe I hope; the fates will find a way: '*Fata viam invenient*'."

But fate did not favor Essy. When Alva died all life seemed to go out of Cap'n Rose. He died before the industry he pioneered got started. The Saint With No Name was beached on Jones's Spit and left to rot away slowly. Some of it is still there.

It is not the stories about Cap'n Rose that stick with me as much as the stories he told. I doubt that he had been more than a hundred miles from home. I'm not sure about Alva, but she was Cape born and I never heard that she had done any traveling. I assume that everything they knew about the world they learned from books, and I assume, too, that Essy came to know so much because Alva shared all she knew with him. And because they seemed to know so much, they are the ones responsible for my reading habits. Books revealed the world beyond Smalltown for me.

Essy had been born and raised in the Catholic Church; I don't know about Alva. Neither went to any church that I know of. It was from Cap'n Rose that I first heard of Buddha in India and Lao-tze in China, first heard the words contemplation and meditation, first learned about Norse gods and Hindu gods. Cap'n Rose drew the direct lines that connected the Athens of ancient Greece to the United States with talk about democracy and the senate and the rights of man. Probably I had heard such things in school, and probably I had not listened, but when Cap'n Rose told the stories, we all listened. He told about Peter, the fisherman, and fishing on Lake Galilee and about the Galapagos Islands and fishing the Amazon. He claimed nothing for himself. "I read" or "I have been told" was his way of explaining his knowledge, or "Did you know...."

Robert Wolley

No one ever doubted his knowledge, which was strange, because everyone in my town was born with a doubting mind, questioning everything and wanting to know by what authority do you substantiate such and such. Not so with Cap'n Rose. His beliefs were Darwinian in implication based on a unification of creation stories from Zulu Indians and Hebrews and Australian aboriginals and who knows what else. We were created, as all things were created, and then we evolved, as all things evolve. We are all a single part of a whole and therefore there should be no division because of race or religion or wealth or whatever. There is God and there are gods, and all are one and the same. It was all very simplistic, but the one thing that stands out was his continued saying that because humans are God's image, we are responsible for each other and for the world.

And that leads me to tell just one story about Cap'n Rose and Alva. When the Great Depression was at its worst, the Roses planted a huge garden. They made it known that anyone who wanted to share the work would share the vegetables. A few people did. Additionally, the Roses stopped selling their fish. Their fish were free to anyone who wanted them. And, finally, the Roses bought a slew of piglets. If anyone wanted to feed and help in keeping the pigs clean, they would share in the slaughter. A few did that, too. But, as hungry as some of us were, and as desperate as some of us were for money to buy food, the majority of people not only refused the Roses' offers but began a whispering campaign against them, calling them communists and other bad names. When the vegetable harvest came around, there was no one to take the food. It went to feed the pigs.

And when the pigs were of a size to slaughter, there was not one taker. Cap'n Rose and his wife took them off somewhere. The word was that they brought home a sizable sum of cash and offered it to the churches and to the American Legion for redistribution, but no one would touch it.

The Pranks An' Enlightenment of Frank An' Me

Talk about absurdities. Here were two saints with the name Rose, and they were rejected. How Cap'n Rose's gods must have wept.

By the time the Roses passed on to Avalon or heaven or wherever they went, all was forgotten. The townspeople had long since recognized their stupidity and had forgiven themselves. I don't know whether they ever forgave the Roses for having shown them what used to be called "the Christian light," doing for others what you would like to have done for you, or, quoting the Persian Zoroastra, as Cap'n Rose did often, "Do as you would be done by."

Robert Wolley

Chapter III

Cloyd, the Rumrunners an' the Sheep

The Pranks An' Enlightenment of Frank An' Me

When Frank and I started school, we had a lot of schoolmates, and at the end of our schooling there were just Frank and me and the Chambers girls. That's because when we started we had mostly Pilot children, Pilot having no school, and such as there were for students came to Smalltown. Later, Pilot folks built their own school, so finally it was just the girls and Frank and me.

Smalltown had its ups and downs. A couple of times more than two thousand people lived here. During the grand whaling days Smalltown was big. My gran'ma's gran'pa built ships here for both whaling and for the packet trade that ran all along the east coast. But when whaling died, so did Smalltown, and when the trains came and made the packets unnecessary, that was like burying the town.

In the 1800s there was a little boom, but it didn't last long, the War of 1812 seeing to that. And what finally nearly finished the town was the Civil War, men going to that horrible conflict and whole families leaving for the factory towns where there was work. Smalltown just got poorer and poorer and the people fewer and fewer until there was but a handful of people and most of them old. People with children just had to move away to feed their families.

By the time I was born, things were a little better, what with the oysters coming back and a dozen or so fishing boats and maybe six or eight scallopers and a few people farming. There was just enough here to keep a couple of hundred people, if that.

You don't see any of evidence of it now, but there used to be a few farms here where people scratched out a living of sorts. I'll tell you something about one farm right here in town and what went on there.

If you hold out three fingers and point them toward the ocean and separate them, you have a perfect map of Smalltown. The pointing finger would be South Smalltown, the middle finger would be Smalltown proper, and the ring finger would be Smalltown Neck. South Smalltown wasn't much, not like it is now, but it had a general store and its own post office. The Neck was mostly all summer folks, what there were of them, and the golf course. I can't remember that any family lived out on the Neck in the winter.

If you keep your three fingers out, the space between the pointing finger and the middle finger would be the harbor, and the space between the middle finger would be called the Meadows, and if you imagine a U running from the harbor and behind the middle finger to the Meadows, you have Main Street where the stores and churches, town hall and post office and all that stuff was. Almost everybody in Smalltown lived around Main Street and down that middle finger, everybody being about two hundred and fifty souls, at least a quarter of them being widows.

Two streets ran down that finger from Main Street. On the south, Fleet Street and on the north, more or less, Depot Avenue. That was always confusing because the train depot was on Fleet Street. But in the whaling days, Depot Avenue went to that section of the harbor where there was a huge row of warehouses for the entire whaling fleet and where oil from the whales was stored. So the name has a reason, long forgotten.

There is some argument about Fleet Street, newcomers wanting to say it's named after a street in London. It isn't, but if it were, it would be kind of high-hat. The truth is, more likely, that because the whaling fleet was at the end of the street, with attendant docks and the refitting area, the street was so named because that is where the fleet was.

About the first knuckle of the middle finger there is a high hill. It falls away gradually to the harbor side, but on the Meadow side it falls off sharply, a cliff about three hundred feet to the bottom. Of course, the hill is just sand, like everything else.

The Pranks An' Enlightenment of Frank An' Me

Now, between Fleet and Depot are a lot of connecting alleys. None of them had names until recently, they being just two-track sand paths leading to people's homes. We lived on the next to last one going to the harbor; Frank lived on the first one right after Main Street, about a half-mile from me. There were three houses on my alley, ten on Frank's, his part of the finger being considerably wider.

The whole Meadows is close to two miles long and over a half-mile wide and long ago undoubtedly was like the harbor except that the whole entrance to the Meadows shoaled in, making a beach and making the Meadows what it is, a murky marsh of muck covered with cattails and marsh grasses.

If I walked from my house to Depot Avenue, I could look down on the Meadows, maybe one hundred feet below. Right up against the side of the cliff, I could look down on the Harris farm. The Harrises farmed on a plot about three-quarters of a mile long and averaging about a hundred yards wide. In a couple of spots where they raised goats and sheep, the farm was somewhat wider.

They planted every conceivable thing and had what Ma called a truck farm, although I don't know why, because the Harrises didn't own a truck. They plowed with a mule and had a horse and wagon.

Lordy, those people worked hard, and spring, summer and fall we bought our vegetables from them, and got goat's milk and cheese and sometimes jelly if Ma ran out of her own.

Sometimes, if I went by Depot Avenue to the fishing boats in the still dark, I'd hear Mr. Harris talking to his mule or working in the barn. He looked to be a hundred and five years old, and in all my years of going to the farm, which wasn't more than five minutes from our house, he never said any more than "Hello, boy" or "Mind yeself, boy." Day or night, I never saw him in his house, always being in the fields or in the barn.

Robert Wolley

Mrs. Harris liked to talk, she being friends with my Gran'ma. She always wore an apron, even in the fields. It had two pockets, one for change, the other for horehound drops which she made herself. She always gave me two, one for now, she said, and the other for later. I never did tell her I hated them. I surely liked Mrs. Harris, and it just didn't seem right to tell a lady who must have been older than her husband that I couldn't stand her candy.

I saw Mrs. Harris a lot because Ma wanted something almost every other day and because sometimes the Harrises would give me a little work, mostly having to do with the sheep and the goats. Mrs. Harris called it "tea-makin'." I called it something else once, and Ma smacked me right on the side of the head.

I got to know the farm well, including the little paths that led all over the Meadows. Some led to the upper end into stands of beach plums and to hills of roses. The plums and rose hips Mrs. Harris used for making jelly. One path went clear across the Meadows to some old cranberry bogs which Mr. Harris still tended and which Mrs. Harris said were first cultivated by the Indians. And one path went to the backside of the beach.

I remember when I first found that path. It started behind the goat pen, and I never would have found it except one day one of the damn goats knocked me through a fence rail, and when he did, I broke the rail and he went like lightning right through the opening and into the trail. I had one 'ell of a time getting him back, I'll say.

Well, here was that path. Some of the time you had to jump from hard place to hard place or else you sank down in muck and water. Where there were really bad places, there were planks stretched out for the walking.

What made the path so mysterious (later I learned that it wasn't a mystery to some others) were the long poles with little nail kegs on one end laid carefully along the path, just resting

The Pranks An' Enlightenment of Frank An' Me

there. Once I got the hang of the path, it didn't take but a few minutes to fetch up on the back side of the beach. I didn't have any use for the path, though, because it landed me a long way from the fishing boats, but I used it a few times just for the fun of it.

I never said anything to the Harrises about the path, not that I was hiding something but because I never thought about it, their paths leading all over and I walking on them.

The Harrises had a son named Cloyd. Funny name; I never knew another with it. Cloyd was about the same age as Ma and Pa, and he and Pa were the closest of friends. Cloyd worked away somewhere but in the summer came home weekends and for a few weeks of vacation. Those times Pa spent a lot of time on the Harris farm with Cloyd. They'd sit out in the fields and shoot crows some days. Pa would neglect his work, which he didn't do much of anyway, either on the beds or taking care of a few businessmen's books. Pa wanted to be a banker, but the most he ever did was a little bookkeeping at the end of each month.

Some nights when Cloyd was in town, Pa came home drunk; some nights he didn't come home at all. This went on for a long time, starting when I was about two. Of course, then I didn't know much, but it went on for years, and later I did know something.

But I did know two things from the first, one being that drink wasn't supposed to be had. It wasn't Ma's or Gran'ma's hard and fast rule, although they both were dead set against drinking as something the devil himself made up; it was the government's rule. But somehow Pa and Cloyd passed around the government. And from the way Pa was sometimes, they must have passed around pretty good. More and more Pa didn't come home and more and more when he did, he had been drinking.

Robert Wolley

The other thing I knew and never dared speak about was the lady friend of Cloyd's that Pa got to liking. I knew Ma knew about her, though, because Ma took to crying a lot, and she and Pa did a lot of arguing. Gran'ma always took me off somewhere when Ma and Pa got that way. And lots of times when Pa was doing his share of yelling, he was drunk, too.

After a while Pa stopped coming home altogether. He spent all of his time at the Harris farm when Cloyd was there, and I don't know where when Cloyd wasn't. After a time, Pa and Ma got divorced, and Pa went off with the other lady. And after that I never saw the other lady.

The Harrises knew what was going on, although they never said anything to me directly. But I could tell.

While Ma and Pa were still fighting and before Pa took himself off for good and I was doing some of the chores for the Harrises and after I found the path to the beach, Pa and Cloyd seemed to come into a sum of money.

Not, we had no inside plumbing of any kind, but Pa all of a sudden got money to bring a pipe inside the kitchen, and if it didn't beat all, he started rebuilding the kitchen, making a little separate room. One day he showed up with a real, brand new hopper, white, with a seat and a cover. He ran another pipe into the new room, and some men showed up and dug a big hole next to the house and lined it with caisson plates. A bigger pipe went from the bottom of the hopper, under the house and into the hole.

In a couple of days our outhouse was gone and we were doing our necessary right there in the house. Pa even had a window put in that little room.

Not long after that some men all dressed in black suits and neckties came looking for Pa. Pa was nowhere to be found.

The Pranks An' Enlightenment of Frank An' Me

Frank said he knew that Pa was hiding out in the Meadows, me and Frank being best friends and Frank's pa knowing everything that was going on everywhere.

One late afternoon a couple of days after that, Cloyd came to the house and said that the Harrises needed the goat pen cleaned out that very day. Cloyd had never come to the house before that that I knew of, but I went because money was money.

About the time I was done scraping and carting off the ten million little bails of stuff, it was almost dark. I looked out over the Meadows to the north and, A'mighty, there was one of those long poles sticking straight up in the air, and beyond that one, I could just make out another.

I was standing there gawking, wondering what was going on, when Cloyd came up. "Ya ain't paid for no lookin'," he said. "And ya ain't paid for no talkin', either," and he handed me a dollar, a whole dollar, four times what Mrs. Harris gave me. "Ya ain't seen no poles never, has ya?" he said.

"No, siree," I answered back. "Not for a whole dollar I ain't."

But of course I told Frank what I had seen. "Markers," he said. "Men come off the rumrunners carryin' liquor an' lug it 'long that there path of yours. Can't see the ground, it bein' dark an' them boxes in the way, so they looks up an' follows them barrels." Frank knew all this, he said, because his pa had told him.

I stayed awake all night figuring I might hear what Frank was talking about, but I didn't. Early the next morning I went to the bluff over the farm, and all the poles, at least the two I saw, were down. I could see Mr. Harris spreading manure on one of his gardens, likely the stuff I had scraped up. And I could hear a lot of noise coming from the barn.

To this day I don't know why I did it, but I just had to see what was in the barn and who was making all the noise. So I went down, and when I went to look through the doors, they were closed. But I peeked between them, and there was Pa and Cloyd and a couple of men I didn't know. They were loading boxes into a truck, the likes of which I had never seen.

I was thinking of going in when Mrs. Harris grabbed my arm and put her hand over my mouth and pulled me away. "Ain't no place for a boy, 'less he wants ta get hurt real bad," she whispered.

I'm not sure what she told me and what Ma told me and what Frank told me because it all got lumped together, but what I got was that Cloyd and Pa and others were transferring liquor that had been brought to the beach in boats and to the farm over the path.

In a way I knew all of that, what with people talking about it and sometimes even hearing the engines of powerful boats in the middle of the night. But hearing stories and really knowing the boats came to the beach and that the stuff was carried over the Harris's path to the barn by your own pa and other people you knew and then was loaded into trucks were two different things. Now I really had seen something.

What I also learned was that Mr. and Mrs. Harris had no heart for it and no part in it, but that didn't turn Cloyd away from the business.

One day Frank said that his pa had given him an A'mighty favorable idea. Next time the poles went up, Frank and I would go and move them so the men carrying the boxes would fall off the path. It would be a little prank on those who were breaking the law.

At the time I didn't think too much about it, except how funny it might be. The next time I saw the poles, I lit out for Frank's and he and I raced down to the beach and entered the path. About halfway along we pulled up a couple of poles. Our original idea was to relocate them, but we weren't strong enough to set the poles back in the much so they'd stay upright. We just left them where we had knocked them over. The idea was coming to be less fun.

We were starting back to the beach because I didn't like the idea of going to the farm when we heard someone coming along the path in the semi-darkness, sloshing in the water and muck because a couple of poles were missing. Whoever it was was swearing something awful.

Now, we couldn't go to the beach. I didn't want to go to the farm, but we had to do something because the voice was getting closer. And familiar! All that swearing was my own pa's. Now, like it or not, we had to move ahead of the voice toward the Harris's. Frank pulled up and knocked down each pole as we went by. I could hear Pa as plain as day in one ear and Frank whispering "Get us out of hear" in the other ear. Pretty soon the men at the farm could hear Pa; they started yelling. Frank and I were between a gunboat and a lee shore.

We couldn't see anything unless we looked up and followed the poles, and in the darkness we weren't exactly sure where we were. I did know that not far before we would get to the goat pen there was a small island of hard ground. If we had a lot of luck, we could detour there, take a little tack inland, and get to the sheepfold. It was all in the pitch black, mind you, and when I thought we were where I wanted to turn off, I miscalculated and we were into muck up to our knees.

The men coming from the farm had a lantern, and at the last second there was just enough light for me to know where I wanted to be. First, though, Frank and I had to lie down flat in the muck behind the cattails, praying we didn't get caught.

That much worked out. Pa met up with the other men and they went off, saying that they had to call off the whole thing for the night.

Maybe the men got their things settled, but Frank and I still had a problem. We finally found our way to the sheepfold. We didn't bother the sheep; they liked having someone around. But when I crawled over the fence, I caught my foot and fell right into their doings. Face first!

Frank came over okay, but I could tell he was holding his nose. Nothing stinks like sheep stuff, and on top stinking muck, I must have smelled all the way to Plymouth. At least that's what Frank said.

Now we were in even more trouble because we weren't home. Ma always tolerated a certain lateness but not hours of it. And there was the matter of the muck and stuff and the smell. Daytime I would have gone swimming, clothes and all, and most of the evidence would have washed off. I considered that even then but decided to go home.

Ma was fit to be tied, the worst I ever saw her, and when I gave her some of the story, she was so mad she couldn't take a whack at me. Funny thing is, Gran'ma got to laughing. She tried to make believe she was mad, too, but she just burst out laughing and pretty soon we're all laughing.

Ma filled the big galvanized tub outside the back door and made me get in, cold water and all. Never before had I taken a bath with Ma holding a lantern. The water was bitter cold for sure, but it was better than the whipping I figured I'd get.

When I finished, Gran'ma washed my clothes. Everything was going to be fine, I figured, but Pa showed up right then, and nothing was right.

It seems one of his cronies saw, smelled more likely, Frank, and when Frank got home some of the men were there to ask what he had been up to. Frank's pa ran the men off soon enough, but not before Frank allowed enough to give the men a pretty good picture. Pa had come home to give me what-for.

I knew he'd wallop me for sure, but somehow Gran'ma got the meanness turned to blaming Pa, and pretty soon he and Ma and Gran'ma were going at it. They forgot all about me. Later I figured it out: that was Gran'ma's scheme all along.

The Pranks An' Enlightenment of Frank An' Me

Word got around town that two boys had bested the rumrunners, and Pa never did carry out his threats to teach me a lesson. Even now I'm not exactly sure what that lesson was going to be.

After that, the Harrises only used me on the farm when Cloyd wasn't there, he being the maddest of all. The first time I went to the farm after that night, Mr. Harris said what he always said, "Hello, boy," but he gave me a hug, and after I helped Mrs. Harris with the goat and sheep tea, Mr. Harris gave me two dollars and sent Ma a big basket of vegetables. "Mind yeself, boy," he said, rubbing my head. He gave Mrs. Harris a little tweak on the cheek and went off somewhere. I could hear him laughing.

Pa hardly ever showed up after that, and I seldom saw Cloyd. Frank's pa said we did more than all the government men put together. I don't know exactly what we did, but whatever it was, people must have liked it because they smiled at us a lot. Least most did. Frank and I kind of liked that.

Robert Wolley

Chapter IV

The Model A, the "Deathmobile" an' the Buick

The Pranks An' Enlightenment of Frank An' Me

The "Deathmobile" was like nothing I had ever seen.

When someone in town died, all I had ever seen was Mr. Peterson's horse-drawn wagon with all the windows so you could see the casket — to make sure it was there, Frank said once.

It wasn't far from the Methodist or Congregational or Catholic churches to the three burying grounds, so people just followed along after the deceased in whatever they had, most walking.

Undertaking was Mr. Peterson's sideline. Some years no one died, and sometimes we'd go a stretch of years. Gran'ma said barbers used to do the undertaking, and the doctors. But Smalltown never had a barber, at least I never knew of one, and old Doctor Hall was never an undertaker because Peterson's father was undertaker before Mr. Peterson. And probably Mr. Peterson's gran'pa, because that's how long the Peterson's had the hardware store. They advertised on their sign being "IN BUSINESS OVER 145 YEARS," if you can believe it, and every year they painted in a new number.

I guess that was true because the Petersons were in the ship hardware business, ship chandlers, way back when ships were built along Bass Creek, long before the railroad came and cut Bass Creek off from the harbor with a dike and a bridge. Long before my memory, that was. Come to think of it, long before Gran'ma's memory, too.

Folks would tell of some poor old relative who had died at sea being temporarily laid away in ice down in a ship's hold, sailing around for months before coming home, and when he got home being laid out proper by the Petersons, so I say Peterson's had been doing undertaking forever, or close to it.

Before Ma married Pa, he tooted around town in one of Mr. Ford's Model T buckboards. When I was small, the old thing was rusting out back. Every now and then Pa would talk about getting it going, but he never did. I remember Ma getting on him because he had let a perfectly good automobile go to pot. By then, of course, Pa had another flivver. He loved automobiles and I guess spent all our money on some kind of tin lizzie or other.

The trouble was, Smalltown only had about five roads with a hard blacktop, everything else being just two wheel paths and ruts or else sand leveled some and covered with oil. Those oiled roads were one of man's worst inventions.

On top of that, where Pa did his oystering and clamming, and the way to get to his favorite spot for beach plum picking, were under water at high tide. Pa never could get the hang of figuring out the tides, and lots of times the water overtook the automobile or else Pa got himself buried in the sand trying to escape the water. Six months of that and all Pa's vehicles looked like moving, when they moved, buckets of rust.

Pa never worked on the fishing boats. No one ever spoke of it, but Pa never was on speaking terms with the water. If you came from generations of seamen and couldn't tell high tide from low, there wasn't much hope. Besides, I expect Pa would have been considered a Jonah on any boat I knew. Just getting near water could get Pa into more trouble than he could handle.

Lucky for Pa, Crane's old wagon shop took to fixing Fords. Thomas Crane used to make a big joke about Pa, saying Pa ought to buy ten miles of rope, tie one end to his flivver and the other end to Crane's shop. Then every hour the Cranes could pull on the rope and drag Pa in because they'd know that Pa was either stuck somewhere or his vehicle was sinking.

Pa never got the humor of it, maybe because it was so true. Anyway, before we got the Model A, Pa was driving out on the flats to his oyster beds. There was a certain route over hard sand and mud, a route established by his gran' uncle who gave him the beds when hauling was done with hand carts and later with horses and wagons. Pa used that route later with the Model T. Everyone who had beds had certain safe routes; to get off such

The Pranks An' Enlightenment of Frank An' Me

routes was to get into soft muck or quicksand. All the routes were marked with dead trees and poles, just as the beds were marked with big trees. It's not so much now, but in those earlier days the harbor was a water forest that was hard to navigate if you left the channel.

Just the week before the time I am going to describe, Mr. Chambers lost his wagon and two horses because one of the horses stepped on something and shied off the path into quicksand. Before enough help could get to Mr. Chambers' rescue, the wagon and horses were gone out of sight.

Pa liked to slew through the little pools of water left by the tide, sending spray all over. Those who saw him that day said he was tooting along as usual when suddenly he skidded and the flivver shot out to the side. It stalled and just sat there off to the side of the safe route, men said, looking forlorn and sad. Pa got out and right off started sinking, finally pulling himself up on the hood of the Model T.

Those who saw what was happening got equipment to help Pa, but it was too late. The Model T was getting smaller and smaller, with Pa sitting on top. Finally, the truck gave off a weird sigh, the men said, gave out a puff of steam, and disappeared, leaving Pa floundering for himself.

When the men secured Pa with a rope and dragged him to hard ground, they said he didn't thank them or anything. All he did was look at the spot where the Model T had gone down, only a few bubbles showing the grave, and said something like, "If I'd knowed the s.o.b. were goin' ta do that, I'd a shot it." And he walked off, refusing all rides.

We didn't know all this until the next day. Pa didn't come home that night, but he had gotten into that habit before then. Ma was worried but said nothing. The next morning Pa drove up in a brand new Model A. Up to then I'd only seen two or three, and they belonged to summer folks, no one in Smalltown, not even Dr. Hall or Peterson or anyone else I knew, being rich enough to own a brand new anything.

Ma took one look at the Model A and burst out crying. Why, she kept asking? Pa looked kind of sheepish. Then he said, as best I remember it, "That there truck were jest too orn'ry; had a mean mind of its own. Had ta let it go." Ma waited for more explanation, but none was forthcoming.

It wasn't for a few days that the meaning of Pa's words came clear. What he said was true enough, if you take the words literally, but the words just didn't do the scene true justice.

Like all of Pa's automobiles, the Model A got old in a hurry. I have no idea why Pa got the thing in the first place, let alone how he was going to pay for it. The second day he had it, he was out on the flats tending his oysters. He loaded up the rumble seat with them, and with lots of muck and seaweed to boot, and by the time beach plum picking was over in September, the thing had so many scratches from driving through the brush that it looked as if someone had taken a clam rake and had spent an entire day giving the outside a going over.

The Model A was old before its time, and when finally it was laid to rest and abandoned, Ma went off Cape to buy another automobile.

By then Pa had gone for good, and Ma had me and Gran'ma to support, which she did by selling magazine subscriptions, giving bridge lessons — that caused a little to-do among the Methodists — and teaching ladies to knit. For all that, she needed transportation. But to tell you the truth, the automobile took more to run and keep in repair than Ma earned.

The fact was that Gran'ma probably earned more in the summer than Ma earned all year, Gran'ma taking to doing laundry and cleaning folks' houses. But she did it quiet-like and put her earnings in the pot and never said anything about it. That was Gran'ma's way.

When Ma did get rid of the Model A, she came back with a

The Pranks An' Enlightenment of Frank An' Me

well-used Oldsmobile. It wasn't your everyday automobile. In fact, it wasn't even a Sunday automobile. It was a faded family funeral car, complete with black curtains with little dangling black balls that could cover all of the rear windows. For sure it was no ordinary automobile; it would have held two Model A editions. It had jump seats in the back and probably carried many a grieving family as they helped a deceased one on his way to the next destination.

Of course, I didn't know it was used to carry weeping people to the grave until folks got to making fun of Ma. I don't think Ma knew what she had until she got home; probably it was the cheapest thing that ran, and that was a cruel joke all by itself.

No matter how fast Ma willed it to go, the Oldsmobile wouldn't go faster than 45 miles an hour. That was okay, since we didn't have roads in Smalltown that allowed such a high speed. But if we went off to P'town or off Cape, there were such roads.

Ma called it a nice family automobile, although Gran'ma was none too happy to be seen riding in it. One day she said something about always riding in a one car funeral procession, and because of that I got to calling it the Deathmobile. Ma hated that.

Naturally, the monster was black, inside and out, except the inside was faded something awful and looked like the gray that gets squeezed out of a stinking mud cod. I offered that opinion just once, followed by a blow that resulted in a ringing in my ear.

Down hill the thing wouldn't get to fifty, that being the large number right at the top of the speedometer, but it would go on forever at two or three miles per hour. I suppose it was geared to a mourner's gait. Maybe to hush all kinds of unpleasant talk, Ma made matters ridiculous by joining the then popular "Not Over 50 Club" and put a big emblem that said that in the back window. She became pretty defensive about the Deathmobile's lack of get up and go, saying that even if the devil himself was chasing her, she would obey the Club's sacred rule.

I guess she must have; years later, long after I had left home, Ma got herself arrested twice on the same day for going too slow. I'm sure the Deathmobile must have had something to do with that.

I knew the Olds was no improvement over the Model A. I told you when my parents got the Model A and why, but after my parents separated, Ma got to keep the Model A as part of the divorce settlement.

Pa had turned it into an old crate by them, and the last year we had it, it wouldn't climb any hill whatever. No matter what, even with the Crane's best efforts, the flivver couldn't make it up a hill of any kind. The last time we made the attempt was to go way down to P'town.

We had a terrible time getting there. Just going through Pamet and Billingsgate was bad enough, and even the little hills were terrible. Gran'ma said we should give it up, but Ma said we were going to have a spring outing. Besides, I needed a haircut and that's where we were going, among other places.

When I heard haircut, I was ready to turn back. A spring haircut always meant getting my head shaved right down to the bare bone. I would look truly stupid, my white head showing as bald as my bottom, Frank used to tell me, and not half as cute. I hated it because the summer girls all made fun of it, for a while at least, until it got tanned and a little bit of blond hair began to show. The only advantage I could ever see was that it meant no haircut until fall.

I got my haircut, we had us a grand time, and we left P'town in good spirits, Ma and Gran'ma in front with the top down and me in the rumble seat. But good times don't last. As soon as we got to the hill leading up to Pamet past Indian Mound Lake, the Model A balked. No way was that A-bucket going to climb that hill. Ma tried three, four times.

The Pranks An' Enlightenment of Frank An' Me

Finally, Ma turned the rust bucket around and backed all the way up the hill, all the way to the top, with other autos looking and gawking and yelling all kinds of mean things. The Model A must have been as embarrassed as we were, which is saying a lot, because once we reached the top and got turned around again, the beast never faltered, even through the towns. But it had had its day.

It didn't seem to matter any to the Deathmobile whether there were hills or not. Up, down, on the flat, it behaved the same. It was nice to ride under cover sometimes; many a trip in the Model A was made trying to keep warm or dry or both in the rumble seat.

But you could love a Model A. Nobody could love a car whose primary reason for being was to accompany the dead to wherever they were going. We used to whoop and holler and sing and have a wonderful time in the Model A; I can't ever remember having a joyful ride in the Oldsmobile. And sad it is but true, we had that car for a long, long time, eight years anyway, and it sure was faithful. But it wasn't ever a happy automobile, and the last time I can remember riding in it was when they buried Gran'ma.

I think Ma knew it was an unhappy car from the first. She got it because she and Pa weren't happy and because he left her to make her own living, and she kept it all those years, I do believe now, to remind herself of the misery. Gran'ma's going was the final misery, and when she went, Ma let the Deathmobile go, too.

I think I felt something of that right from the beginning when Pa left with the summer lady. Once in a while he'd come to fetch me, mostly on summer Saturdays, because the judge said he should.

So, every Saturday for a while after their divorce, I'd sit on the front stoop waiting for my father. Most times he never came.

Robert Wolley

I stopped sweeping Mr. Peterson's store just to make sure my Pa didn't miss me. After lots of disappointments, Mr. Peterson let me sweep real early in the morning. Sometimes he let me sweep late Friday.

When my pa did come for me, he'd give me a dime for an allowance. If several weeks had gone by without his visits and payments, which was usually, then I might receive a big sum all at once.

There was a catch, however. I had to earn the allowance, and the way I earned it was to play a betting game. I had to wager double or nothing. For a couple of years the double or nothing game became a ritual.

Pa would drive up to the house; I would be greeted with the obligatory kiss and climb into the front seat of his Buick.

Off we'd go for a ride, sometimes just around town, sometimes to Barnstable to one of Pa's brother's houses. I was never let into that house because Pa's brother's wife thought I was too rough and dirty for my cousins, so I had to wait in the Buick until Pa got through his visiting. Sometimes we'd go to the golf course. Pa had begun playing golf with the summer people, and he made me chase balls for him.

Pa never said much and I'm not sure the four or five visits each year were all that much fun, but I loved my pa and fervently wished things had been different between him and Ma. And I loved sitting in the front seat of the Buick.

Right when Pa left and took up with the summer lady, he had a Buick. Maybe it was hers, I don't know, but every year there was a new one. I knew Pa had no money for one, but then he moved up to Boston and must have done work there. He sold his oyster beds, but they weren't worth much. They were worth what work a man put into them. I wanted him to give one bed to me, but he wouldn't.

The truth is, Pa never gave me anything except once he gave me a brand new bicycle. I'd never even been on a bicycle, there

The Pranks An' Enlightenment of Frank An' Me

not being places to ride one. I had to learn by myself on the dirt roads, and between the sand and failing off mostly, the thing looked just like one of Pa's flivvers.

Anyway, wherever we'd be going, we'd be on a road. That's when the betting game began. My Pa would bet me double or nothing for my allowance that I couldn't tell him when we'd gone a mile or two miles. Or he would bet me double or nothing that he could guess better than I could how far we had gone in ten minutes.

He would put his hand over the odometer and we'd make our guesses some minutes later. Pa always won. I was poor at the game; most of the time I was poor when he took me home. A couple of times he gave me the dime anyway, but most of the time I was left penniless. For a couple of years I had an allowance that I never got.

I remember that it was just a couple of months before my twelfth birthday when I figured it out, or someone told me, or Pa let the secret slip. I really don't remember how I learned the secret; that's one thing I can't remember about the whole business.

But suddenly I knew. I knew when we'd gone a mile, or two miles, or even half a mile. If my guesses weren't any better than Pa's, at least they were just as good.

There are forty telephone poles in a mile. I never told Pa I knew that, just a couple of times took my allowance double. But after my twelfth birthday, Pa didn't come around anymore, and there was no more allowance.

Pa used to come to Smalltown, though, because sometimes I'd see a Buick at the Harris farm. Pa and Cloyd were always best friends. I don't think the summer lady ever came back because no one ever said so. And a few years later we heard that Pa had left her and got himself a new lady. It wasn't until I was older that I learned that Pa traded ladies for a while about as often as he traded automobiles.

Robert Wolley

Chapter V

Party Lines

The Pranks An' Enlightenment of Frank An' Me

Having thought about it, maybe I do remember where I got the fine knowledge that allowed me to beat Pa at his double or nothing game.

It was undoubtedly unconscious on my part at the time, but the summer of my twelfth birthday, the telephone company had a huge expansion and Frank and I pulled off one of our greatest pranks.

I mean the expansion was big. There were never more than eighty-six telephones in Smalltown up to the year I was twelve. And I mean the greatest prank because it was.

All this is connected together: Pa's game, the telephone business, and the prank.

By the summer of my twelfth birthday, Smalltown had become a fashionable place for summer people. I didn't blame the people for coming to Smalltown; it was a wonderful place in which to live, even if we who lived here had a hard go of it. Smalltown wasn't always poor, once being almost ten times as large, but for years hard times were the rule. Then people started to come for the summer, buying up old unused houses or building new ones in the woods or on the Neck, and I guess all those people wanted to have telephones.

Up on the north end of Main Street, Hattie Chase, Gran'ma's cousin, so I called her Aunt Hattie, ran the telephone company in her living room. She was the only operator, so she hardly ever left her house. And if she did, she had Gran'ma as the operator.

We didn't have a telephone; hardly anyone did, but two or three of our neighbors did, nice old Miss Harper, who lived down the end of our alley on Depot Street, and the Widow Cressey, who lived on the hill above the Harris farm, and the two inns on Fleet Street.

I had never used a telephone in a house until I was past fourteen, but I used to go to Miss Harper's house a lot because I carried her groceries from the First National store every Friday afternoon. I never was in Mrs. Cressey's house.

Miss Harper's telephone was nailed on her living room wall, a little yellow wooden box, oak most likely, with a mouthpiece sticking out above two little bells. An earpiece hung to one side; there was a crank on the other side. Miss Harper's ring was 3-3. That is, if someone wanted to speak with Miss Harper, Aunt Hattie rang the bell three times, with a little pause, then three more times. The first three rings were for a section of the line; the second three were Miss Harper's own number on that part of the line.

Of course all eighty-six telephones didn't ring at the same time. There were eight main lines radiating out of Aunt Hattie's with various numbers of telephones on each line. The main lines were separated somehow into secondary lines. When someone was called, all the phones on that part of the line rang even though only one person was wanted, so when a phone was in use, a lot of people could listen in, and did, including Aunt Hattie.

She had a thing in her living room that looked like an upright piano, only where the keys might have been were wires coming up with big plugs on the end. These she plugged into holes in front of her. Each wire was someone's telephone and each hole was someone's telephone, all bound together in sublines and mainlines and by Aunt Hattie and her switchboard.

Every week on Thursday, a dozen ladies played cards at Aunt Hattie's house. They called it their "Sewin' Circle" because some, like Ma and Gran'ma were supposed to be against card playing, being Methodists, you know. I don't think the Catholics and the Congregationalists had the same view, but it was always the Sewing Circle anyway.

I do believe that every telephone call made since the week before was relayed to the other ladies by Aunt Hattie. Ma and Gran'ma would talk between themselves about it for days. There

The Pranks An' Enlightenment of Frank An' Me

were no secrets in Smalltown, because between Aunt Hattie, the telephone and the Sewing Circle, secrets got around faster than lightning. A lot of the ladies of the Sewing Circle thought they were safe from being reported, but Aunt Hattie was truly democratic when it came to telling Gran'ma things.

When it was Ma's or Gran'ma's turn to provide refreshments for the ladies, I had to carry them to Aunt Hattie's.

Now, that was a blessing in disguise. First, Aunt Hattie always gave me some candy, sometimes a couple of pennies, and usually a nice drink of birch beer which she had made herself. But best of all, over time she taught me how to operate her switchboard. She said she taught everybody how, because for some reason, whenever someone came to her house, she always had to go to the necessary, and it wouldn't do for a call to be unanswered. And I do think that dozens of folks knew how to work the thing.

Someone wanting to make a call gave one twist of their crank. That rang the switchboard, one ring being for Aunt Hattie. You could ring the other folks on your line just by ringing their particular rings, but you couldn't bypass Aunt Hattie because her switchboard rang, too. And on her rows of plugs a tiny light would shine, indicating which line was in use.

When the switchboard rang and the light came on, Aunt Hattie would take the right plug and shove it in the main hole. Then she'd ask who you wanted to talk to. When whoever it was gave the name, a little card tacked on to the side said which hole got plugged in. Say someone wanted to talk with Miss Harper. Put the plug in her line hole, turn the crank three plus three times and Miss Harper would answer.

When she did, Aunt Hattie was supposed to unplug from the main hole, the little lights telling her that the connection was complete. When one of the lights went out, the call was ended. But Aunt Hattie seldom unplugged herself, and that was how she

Robert Wolley

knew so much about Smalltown. And that was how I knew so much.

There were sixty houses, maybe, that had telephones, including Dr. Hall and the pastors of the churches. And there were telephones in the stores, Peterson's and the First National and the fish market and others, one for each of the post offices, one for the Coast Guard station, perhaps five in the town hall. Then there was the dock master's office on the fish pier, and the bank, and one in the fire station, and a few others I don't remember. No matter.

The summer I was twelve, telephone poles started going up all over the place, hundreds of them. Aunt Hattie said that everybody in town was going to have a telephone, although we never did. But the worst thing possible, said Aunt Hattie, was that the telephone company was going to build an exchange, whatever that was, just two doors from her house, and bring in new operators, and she would lose her job.

Maybe with all the hole digging and everything is how I came to know that there were forty telephone poles to a mile. Maybe. I can't remember exactly if that's how I came to know that, but it's as good an explanation as I have.

Anyway, the new exchange was unsettling news to Aunt Hattie and to my gran'ma because Gran'ma got a few dollars from helping out Aunt Hattie. But at the same time, all the activity provided some interest to Frank and me. We got to collecting scraps of wire and glass knobs and big spikes and did a lot of watching. Frank got to watching more than I did because some mornings before five o'clock I'd go down to the fishing boats and hope that one of the fishermen would give me a day's work. Sometimes they did; most times they didn't, but usually twice a week I'd get to go out, so I had to keep trying, poor times being what they were.

Frank and I got to know some of the men who were stringing up the wires, and they let us listen in on the lines they

The Pranks An' Enlightenment of Frank An' Me

were putting up. They talked with each other miles away to test the lines and to amuse each other.

Sometimes when a wire was going to a house, we got to do the talking for one of the men. Maybe that's how we got started on our prank. Maybe. I don't remember just how we got started, but somehow the telephone in the fire station got our attention.

It was plumb foolish to have one in the fire station because no one was ever there, Smalltown having but one fire engine and a volunteer fire department. The only time anyone was in the station was when there was a fire or just after.

The town had three fire whistles, one on the town hall, one on the fire station, and one on the South Smalltown Post Office building. They could be rung by anyone who needed help, and when they were rung, everyone rushed to the fire station. When the location of the fire or emergency was determined, from the fire station all alarms would be rung in a kind of code telling the location of the trouble, and if you didn't go to the station, you could go to the trouble directly.

Because of the volunteer fire department and the need to get the engine out fast, the station was never locked. The first man there opened the doors, started the truck and usually drove away as soon as a second man appeared. There were times when an eager driver took off before he knew where he was supposed to go.

There was a lot of competition for driving the truck. More than once there were fistfights over who was going to drive, and more than once fires that might have been put out didn't get put out because the fight lasted too long.

I remember one Saturday morning. I was cleaning up at Peterson's, and the whistle blew. The fire station was almost across the street, which meant that Peterson usually got to drive the fire engine.

Robert Wolley

But that morning, John Peterson was selling something to Amos Spring. When the whistle went off, they both rushed out the door. First, they got to the door at the exact same time, and right off they started punching each other. They were hauling at each other all the way across the street. Then, while they were doing that to each other, Johnny Atwood appears, gets the fire station doors open and gets in the driver's seat and cranks up the fire truck.

Well, that gets Mr. Peterson and Mr. Spring madder. Both began yelling at Johnny to get down from the fire truck, and when he didn't, they yanked him down, and the three of them were all wrapped up in wrestling.

By then other men came along, and it took some time to get the three separated and the longest time to get the fire engine to the fire. Mr. Spring was so mad that he said he'd never use Peterson's again, which he didn't, I guess, for a long time, but after a while it all got patched up.

The fire that day was at Grace Willis's. She was one of Smalltown's widows. She lived out on a little road behind the schoolhouse in a funny little Cape Cod house, really old. It had just two rooms downstairs, a sitting room and a kitchen, with a bedroom above.

When the fire's location was determined, I ran all the way up to see it. Got there before the fire engine, I did, and the house was going up pretty good. Someone, though, was up in the bedroom yelling for people to catch valuables that he was going to throw out the window. First came two pillows. Than out came a big mirror. Then two oil lamps. Of course, no one caught the mirror and the lamps, both crashing into pieces on the ground.

Miss Willis was yelling for this precious piece or that, but I guess nothing was saved. Other breakable stuff came flying out the window with predictable consequences. I didn't know who was doing the throwing until Jess Potter's head appeared in the

The Pranks An' Enlightenment of Frank An' Me

window. He yelled that he couldn't get out because the flames were now in the bedroom and would someone please put up a ladder.

But first, he was going to save Miss Willis' most valuable objects. Out came a night chamber pot. Crash. Then out came Miss Willis' cat. That was a sight, both flying through the air and landing. And then out came a pair of bloomers, and another, and another. All of Miss Willis' most personal underclothes came floating down, one at a time.

Now, Jess never was Smalltown's most intelligent person. How he got into the house in the first place was a mystery, but apparently enough was enough, and the men decided to get him out before he got hurt and before Miss Willis died of mortification.

When Jess got to the ground, he stood with his arms up and yelled to the crowd, "I's saved everythin' o' Miss Willis's worth." The cat couldn't be found, but except for the two pillows and some unmentionables, everything Jess had tossed out was in tiny pieces. When someone pointed that out to him, he said, "That you' fault. I done my savin'."

What with the fighting at the fire station and the long delay and then standing around watching Jess save the contents of Miss Willis's house, there was no fire fighting and the house burned to the ground.

But I've jumped off the track, haven't I? Later I'll tell you more about Jess Potter and how Miss Willis got her new house. You'll want to know all about that.

But now I want to get back to the telephone men. Maybe because the telephone men made up some outlandish stories when they were talking on the lines, like "Mad dog heading your way; looking for raw dark meat!" (Some of the men told us they had come from the Carolina and Georgia islands.) Frank and I had a riotous time some days. There was a lot of teasing. "Now, take the wire an' shove it in your ear. If ya don't hear nothin' the wire be good but you brain ain't." Of course, when something went wrong there was a lot of swearing, but it was mild compared to what we heard on the boats when something was amiss.

The telephone men, when they were talking on the wires, commented about every living thing that went by, people and animals. It was, to say the least, an education in the males' apprehension of the world.

After listening to all that for weeks, Frank put everything together and said we ought to do something that would wake up the ladies when they were at Aunt Hattie's.

That's when we considered the fire station because we knew that was the one telephone we could get to. I think Frank had a plan all worked out and just strung me along, hauling me in like a cod that had swallowed hook, line and sinker. He knew what we ought to do to excite the ladies, but patient-like, he let us discuss it for a week or more.

Now, Aunt Hattie was a widow like a lot of ladies in the town, and she was used to emergencies, especially for Dr. Hall and the fire department and the Coast Guard, so what we had to do was create something that would get her and the other ladies real excited. We thought of fire, ship wrecks and sinkings and other accidents. None of them seemed good.

Frank came up with the idea, which I do believe he had all along. We'd be someone come back from the dead. We'd make believe we were someone who had died and, like some comic book characters, had to come back to life to take care of something. We needed someone good, someone who....and Frank just happened to know who that person should be: Mary Greentree.

There used to be Indians around here, lots of them, I suppose, but I knew only one, Mary Greentree. She used to come

The Pranks An' Enlightenment of Frank An' Me

to our school and tell about real Cape Indians, and when she died that was the last of the full-blooded Indians in Smalltown.

There were people with Indian blood hereabouts, some down Billingsgate way. They weren't whooping and hollering Indians. What I mean is that they were Indians who had gotten their blood mixed with Negroes who came here after the Civil War or with folks who came from the Canary Islands or from Cape Verde or from Portugal, and after a while who knows what anyone was, especially when so many were married to Cape children. People used to say that all the Indians were gone, but that's not so. Indians are still here, but they are mingled with the rest of the population. It is sad that the Indians' part has been lost. There are a few who try now and then to bring out some of the old Indian culture, but most aren't full-blooded Indians. When I was a boy, Mary Greentree was the last and never until I came back after I left here was there anyone else who claimed to be a full-blooded Indian. Not here, anyway, not around here. Up Cape, maybe, and on the islands, but not here.

Frank had a most wonderful notion when he came up with Mary Greentree. So Mary Greentree it would be.

Before she died, Mary had claimed to be over a hundred and ten years old. She lived on the Pilot line somewhere in the swamp. I never saw her place, but it must have been on one of the wooded rises that were in Big Swamp. Frank and I knew two kinds of things about her, facts and fancies. She had a small farm and trapped and hunted. She made deerskin boots and shirts and sold them along with shell jewelry at a summer stand. She was old, all bent over. And she was smart, sometimes coming to school to tell us about Indians and their lives. For all her peculiar ways, she was wonderful to have in school.

And she was a fortuneteller, too, but only told fortunes at night. She told people things she couldn't possibly have known. Folks were a little scared of her because she knew the future. Frank and I used to call her a witch, but not to her face, and surely not because we didn't like her, but she was mysterious, and it seemed to us, possessing knowledge only a witch could know.

Mary Greentree could read and write. After she died, Dr. Hall revealed to the town that Mary had been educated in a woman's seminary somewhere in New Jersey and had taught school for a couple of years shortly after the Civil War somewhere in Canada. So she must have been nearly as old as she claimed. She was born sometime between 1848 and 1850 in or near Concord, Massachusetts, on a trading post. Since she was an Indian, no record of her birth exists, but her diploma is in the historical society along with her teaching certificate.

When she came to school to tell us about Indians, she read papers she said were all wrong about the Indians, and then she set us right. She knew a lot. She wrote stuff on the blackboard, names of places she'd been because she said she'd been in the whale boats. That may be how she ended up in Smalltown. She never did tell us about that.

When she came to school, she always had something to tell about the families that had been on the Cape for a long time, and she would tell us what was going to happen to us. That was scary.

One day she told Frank that he would die a young man, and he did in World War II; she told me I'd journey far away and leave most of what I loved behind, and to my sorrow I did; she told Miss Barney, our teacher, she would have to give up teaching, and she did because she got herself a baby and people made her move away.

That was Mary Greentree's hold on the town. She told what sooner or later came to be true. People, mostly women, were afraid of her, yet they kept inviting her to tell their fortunes.

Mary had died about seven months before. We had had a bad, terribly cold, long winter, and she was found on the steps of town hall, frozen to death.

The Pranks An' Enlightenment of Frank An' Me

So Mary Greentree would make a call to the ladies playing cards at Aunt Hattie's.

It was easy to think of something for "Mary" to say to Ma and Gran'ma and Aunt Hattie and Frank's ma. We had to do some snooping for the other ladies.

A few of the ladies, like Ma and Gran'ma, were devout Methodists, and card playing was not considered the best way to get into heaven. I guess the Congregationalists never cared about it. And the Catholics, like Frank's ma, what there were of them, played cards right in their own church. Now, we used to hear that there were all kinds of nets thrown up between people of one church or another. That wasn't so in Smalltown. No Catholic this or Protestant that. Many a Catholic and Protestant were in equal shares with a boat. No black this or Indian that or Cape Verdean the other. Maybe we were too dumb to make the differences important, or maybe we just had such a time of getting by that all that stuff never got in the way.

Perhaps the pastors didn't take to it, their business being to save souls according to their particular beliefs, but a lot of people were like Aunt Hattie. She was of no church. Sometimes she went to the Catholic church. "When I feels the need for a little upliftin'," she would say. Easter and Christmas she simply unplugged all the telephone lines and went to one or the other of the Protestant churches. She'd complain about not understanding a word in the Catholic church, but that was about the only criticism I can remember. She was truly a universal spirit. Maybe knowing everybody and talking with so many every day, she figured we weren't so different and were all under the same Almighty.

Well, we had this good idea but didn't know what to do with it. Frank would call and be Mary Greentree. Aunt Hattie would take the call and we figured she'd be just too smart to fool. "Mary" couldn't talk with Aunt Hattie, else we would be done before we started. We couldn't talk with Gran'ma because she knew Mary too well.

But there was Miss Rich. She was younger than most of the other ladies, and she had lived a strange life, according to Ma and Gran'ma. It seems she had been engaged to be married at different times to two men, both of whom ran off with someone else, each leaving Miss Rich with a ring and a promise and nothing else.

Perhaps that is why Miss Rich was dead set against men. The word was that she was one of Mary's best customers for a while and that Mary had told her once that no man was going to come and court her and that she should give herself to the Lord.

The story goes that Miss Rich gave away everything, which surely couldn't have been much, and went off to Boston or some other place. She came back in a few weeks. It seemed that no convent had a place for a Congregationalist women who hated men, no matter how much she wanted to serve the Lord.

Miss Rich worked in the Smalltown tax office, and that gave her all the time in the world to be mean to males. I mean, Miss Rich was mean to any male, young or old, and we often rhymed her name in songs we made up, she being the main target.

Now we had ourselves a natural victim. Frank got on the fire station telephone that day, and he surely could sound like Mary Greentree. Right off he asked for my ma. I only got his side of the conversation. It started out like we rehearsed it. We didn't want to start right in on Miss Rich.

Pretty soon Frank was off on his own. "Agatha, this be ya only chance," Frank was saying. Agatha was Ma's Christian name, a name she truly detested and which no one called her for fear of severe consequences. Ma went by her middle name, Anne. "Agatha," Frank went on, "I's talked directly with the Lord an' He's angry with ye."

Right there I figured Frank had spoiled it. Whoever said "ye?" But Ma must have let it go right by and asked questions

The Pranks An' Enlightenment of Frank An' Me

because Frank went on, "Ye (that word again) knows playin' cards is against the Lord's way." There was a pause. "This be Mary Greentree. I 'specially wants ta talk with Agnes Rich." There was a long pause. I figured Ma had caught on. Later I would know that she was thrown off guard by being called Agatha. Then I heard Frank say, "I don't need no telly-phone, Harriet. I got the power ta hear an' see all. Right now I sees ya makin' hard drink in ya cellar. I sees ya making them unnatural looks at the telly-phone man ya calls Samuel."

Lordy, I didn't know either of those facts, but they must have been true. Old Aunt Hattie making booze was one thing; old Aunt Hattie working to net a man was beyond belief.

But Frank keeps up. "Pull ya plugs if ya wants, but keep listenin'. I's goin' ta talk with Agnes Rich 'cause I mightn't have another chance."

To this day I don't know why Aunt Hattie never caught on. She knew which line the call was on. Only eight or nine telephones were on that line, Dr. Hall, the bank, Petersons, the fire station, the First National, the wharf master's, and the two inns, Child's and Cole's. There were no homes on that line at all. Even Dr. Hall's residence telephone was on another line.

Perhaps the whole thing caught Aunt Hattie by surprise because pretty soon there was Frank talking with Agnes Rich.

"Agnes," he said, making like Mary Greentree, "I sees somethin' I must tell ya." Pause. "Ye alone." Another pause. "Agnes Rich, no talkin'; jest listen. I be wrong when I was with ye on earth. I be wrong when I says no man'll ever come callin' on ye. Never was I wrong 'fore or after, but up here (with emphasis on the up word) I sees my one mistake. Agnes Rich, today a man will enter ya life. I knows ye will be mean as ye always are. Listen ta me, Agnes. Open your heart ta this man, throw ya arms wide, smother him with kisses. Be a woman."

Robert Wolley

Frank was sweating something awful. But he had a grin a mile wide. He was reciting some of the stuff we had read in magazines we'd found on the beach. I came close to death when he told Miss Rich to undo a couple of buttons on her blouse. Now, I remember saying to myself, he's done it for sure, but Miss Rich must have loved it because Frank didn't quit. But I knew he was in over his head.

Thank the Lord he must have known it, too. Pretty soon he says she'll never hear from "Mary" again, wouldn't have except Mary had to set her one mistake right. Frank ended with a long, drawn out "goooooood byeeeee."

When Frank hung up the telephone, we lit out of the fire station as fast as our legs could manage and ran along the creek, putting distance between ourselves and the station.

The most we figured would come of it, even if everything went as planned, was that the ladies would have something to talk about for a bit. Then they would recognize a prank. They might even suspect us, but if we were careful, they'd never know for sure. If worse came to worse, we'd try to direct the whole thing to all the telephone men around town. And if that didn't work, well, we hadn't planned that eventuality.

But when I got home, Ma and Gran'ma paid me no mind at all. They were filled with talk about Mary Greentree and Agnes Rich. The fact is, they were pure giddy, and when Ma kissed me goodnight, I could smell liquor. Aunt Hattie must have let the ladies sample her secret stuff.

Frank and I went out of our way to avoid all the ladies who were at Aunt Hattie's that day. Frank said his pa was so mad at his ma for drinking that his pa sent her to bed. Husbands used to exercise that authority. There was no supper in Frank's house that night, and Frank got a lecture an the evils of the world, some evils he said we ought to try because his pa made them sound so good.

The Pranks An' Enlightenment of Frank An' Me

When I took Miss Harper's groceries to her the next day, she was on the telephone. By Saturday, everyone in town knew that Mary Greentree had spoken from the dead, and that was all anyone talked about. Most people knew that none of it was true, but no one wanted to come right out and say so. Mary Greentree was no more, but she had a hold on the town that couldn't be let go.

I'm not sure what happened to Miss Rich immediately after that because I didn't see her for a time. I know her man never showed up because there was no man, but Ma and Gran'ma talked about her changing her ways and spending a lot of time down in P'town where there were thousands of people in the summer and where there were lots of single men and women. Frank's pa said it was a city of sin and one day the Lord was going to wipe it off the face of the earth, just like He did with Gomorrah and Sodom.

The rest of the summer was all taken up with Mary Greentree and Agnes Rich. Even the fishermen talked about Miss Rich, not always in wholesome ways, although much of what they said went over my and Frank's head. But the idea of it was not lost on us, the general opinion being that Miss Rich might have made a man a fruitful wife.

It wasn't until winter that I saw Miss Rich; maybe it was late fall. Anyway, it was by accident. I was at the town hall, so it must have been November, paying Ma's tax bill, when there she was, standing at the town clerk's counter with a man. When she saw me, I wished to hide, but she called me by name and told the man what a good lad I was, saying how I helped my ma and earned money and all.

She sure looked differently, too. Her hair was cut short, lips and cheeks colored the way the summer girls colored theirs, and wearing bright clothes. She looked like a girl almost.

She said she was getting marrying papers for Christmas and that she and James, that was the man's name, would be married in Smalltown before they moved to someplace I have forgotten in New York state.

By the time I got home, with a little detour to Frank's, Ma already knew about Miss Rich and her James. Gran'ma was speculating on whether Miss Rich would have children.

"Too ol'," Ma was claiming.

"Not," said Gran'ma. "Woman like that bottled up all these years will s'prise ya. Wait an' see. She'll have a slew of kids, catchin' up fo' lost time."

That argument went on forever, even after Miss Rich got married. I never did know the fact of it, but Miss Rich being woman enough, as Gran'ma put it, kind of ended the whole thing.

By February, most of the telephone work was done. Aunt Hattie said that by summer she'd be out of a job, but it wouldn't matter. After all her years of being a widow, she was going to marry Samuel Dane, one of the telephone men.

When I asked Ma how many children she thought Aunt Hattie would have, she gave me a lick.

"Boy," she said, "don't ya ever ask 'bout a sixty-year-ol' woman." She was mad.

I didn't understand how she could speculate about Miss Rich and not about Aunt Hattie. Gran'ma set me straight; at least I think she did.

We were sitting at the table eating supper when Gran'ma looked at Ma and said, "The boy needs a father. Heard he was askin' ya a question an' ya licked him. Right he should ask, 'cause it be natural, an' right ya should give an answer, 'cause he ain't got no father ta answer him." Ma said nothing.

"Truth be," Gran'ma said, looking at me, "when a woman gets long in years, she can't have no babies no more. Aunt Hattie's too ol'; I'm too ol'. Ya ma ain't, though, jest like Agnes Rich. Still time."

The Pranks An' Enlightenment of Frank An' Me

Ma looked distressed, and when Gran'ma delivered her last line on the subject, Ma took flight out the back door. I don't remember the exact words because of Ma's hollering at Gran'ma, but Gran'ma said something about liking to try landing fish even when you knew the hook wasn't baited.

Robert Wolley

Chapter VI

Some Smalltown Folks

The Pranks An' Enlightenment of Frank An' Me

Divorce was so rare in those days, at least going through the legal business of it, that it wasn't for years that I ever heard of another. Most of her life, Ma told people who didn't know differently that she was a widow; shamed, I expect. Some people, out of hearing, of course, called her a grass widow. It wasn't until I was older that I knew just what that meant.

Ma and Pa's divorce was hard on me in some ways. Ma was good and Gran'ma was wonderful, and the town folks were especially good. Many there were who went out of their way to be particularly kind to me. My early teens was when I missed having a pa the most.

I seldom saw Pa after my twelfth birthday. Later, when I was older, I tried to see him, but it was pointless. And later I found out that he had officially disowned me. By then he had other children and had become well off. I guess he was afraid that I would want some of his money. I never did; all I ever wanted was a father.

Ma never remarried. She should have. Things have changed so much that if you aren't divorced these days, you're the odd one. Or so it seems.

I can truthfully say that I never got into real trouble. Nor did Frank. Mischief plenty, but not bad trouble. Couldn't. Couldn't turn around without someone knowing it. A wonderful thing then, people watching out for everybody else. Maybe life was not private enough for some, but nearly every person cared enough about every other person, man, woman and child, to watch out. No, more than that, to watch over.

And who could I get into trouble with? Frank? There was no one else. What could we steal? No one had anything. There were no opportunities, that's for sure, but there were the occasional temptations to do pranks, some of which I have told you about.

Robert Wolley

Was life simpler back then? Maybe. There was more caring, that's for sure. Perhaps it was simpler for grown-ups because they spent all their time scratching for a living. There was little time for much else. Frank and I, because we were almost a whole male generation, were different from children now. We went to school, but we also worked, and by the time I was fourteen, I was working a man's full hours and still getting in my classes.

Still, we played and played lots up to that time.

When I was eight, Ma rented a skiff for me from Mr. Prince. I rowed it for a year, then Ma rented an outboard motor to go with it. The motor was gigantic and heavy and used a lot of gasoline. I don't remember the horsepower; probably about four or five. It was a boat and motor, but it never was anything but a toy and an expensive one at that.

When I cleaned Mr. Peterson's store, the pay was ten cents. Then, a gallon of gasoline cost nine cents, and I had a penny left over for candy. When gasoline went to eleven cents a gallon, Mr. Peterson didn't raise my wages none, and there wasn't any more candy for me.

Unless one is old enough, wages and prices from back then appear to be ridiculously low. Remember, a well-paid school teacher might get six or seven hundred dollars a year, a store clerk four or five cents an hour, a doctor two dollars a visit. A double ice cream cone or a Moxie or a loaf of bread could each be bought for a nickel. A whole house could be rented for a year for three hundred dollars, about the cost of a new Model A. A haircut cost five cents. So, if you had a few dimes in your pocket, you had big money; even a penny had considerable value.

I had to lug the gasoline for the outboard motor nearly two miles, unless someone gave me a lift, but gasoline cost a lot more on the wharves. Gasoline was hand pumped in those days, so when I pumped it, I sometimes managed to get in a little extra. I guess Mr. Peterson knew that; he always asked me if I had pumped a full gallon, which if I had meant that I owed him a

The Pranks An' Enlightenment of Frank An' Me

penny. I always carried my gasoline in a two gallon pail, so it was hard to tell whether I had cheated Mr. Peterson out of those few extra drops, but I noticed that if he pumped the gasoline for me, there was always a bit more than a gallon. Sometimes he'd just say, "Oh, hell, boy, just fill it up and have yourself a good time."

Mr. Peterson would never take anything for a length of fishing line or for hooks and sinkers. It's an investment, he'd tell me. At first I didn't know what he meant; later I hoped that he had been repaid, although in one regard I know that I had disappointed him. The Petersons never had children, so there was no one to carry on. More than once he told me that I might work in his store someday. Again, at the time, I didn't realize what he was suggesting, if he was suggesting anything, because I'm just taking his suggestion and assuming that I might have been welcome later in life to be his partner.

But what youngster thinks about such things or even remembers them? Not I, anyway, and if I had thought about it, the undertaking part of the business would have scared me off. Some years after I had left Smalltown, I stopped to see him. He was getting old. "Time to be givin' up, son. Thought maybe one day I'd see ya 'hind the counter." That's when I realized that he might have made me an offer when he spoke so many years before.

I loved the skiff; it was just right for a kid. Then one day, Mr. Prince showed me a catboat he said my gran'pa had made. He said it had been in his barn for years. If Ma wanted to rent it for me, he would put it in the water and see that it was rigged properly.

I hadn't known about that particular boat before then. Mr. Prince told me that he had bought it new for mackerel fishing for one hundred fifteen dollars, including the sail. Gran'ma said that Gran'pa sometimes made two such boats a winter for men who would come to his shop and do some of the work themselves.

She thought such a low price meant that Mr. Prince had done a lot of the work and had probably provided a lot of the lumber, especially for the keel, knees and bow stem, since heavy white oak was not readily available on the Cape.

When I asked Mr. Prince about that, he said that what was used were a lot of timbers from the ships that fetched up on the back shore. "There for the takin'," he said.

There were lots of boats stored in barns and under barns and houses. And, of course, boats were left to rot all over the shore, some of them mighty good boats, too. There was a time when it was cheaper and easier to build a new boat than to have a wrecked one repaired.

I got the catboat. I might never have known about it had Frank's pa's boat not been wrecked. Frank's pa owned a sailing dory, and we'd been learning to sail forever. But it was a slow scow and took two to sail, least two small boys. I could row the skiff faster than that dory, I think.

The catboat came up in the first place because the dory got shoved in. It wasn't our fault, but one day we left her tied behind Cap'n Joyce's big fishing boat, which was tied to the south wharf. Someone came in to tie behind the cap'n's boat, paid no mind to the dory, and when he did, crushed it against the pilings. Some summer fellow. He paid twenty dollars for the dory, but of course you couldn't get anything for that, and because Frank's pa was crippled, he didn't ever get anything else.

But Frank's pa did give the twenty dollars to Ma to help pay the rent on the catboat, and I gave up the rowboat with its outboard. Ma had paid twenty dollars a year to Mr. Prince for the skiff and another twenty for the outboard. Mr. Prince got fifty dollars for the catboat and two more dollars for painting the bottom, so Ma made eight dollars the very first year.

Some folks now think that nine or ten is pretty young to have boats and motors and sailboats, but no one ever thought as much then. For us, boats were like bicycles for city kids or like

The Pranks An' Enlightenment of Frank An' Me

country kids running farm vehicles. Sailing was like walking. It was natural.

The trouble with the catboat, though, was at ten I was too small to raise the sail; the gaff was so heavy. Frank and I together could just manage it. When I was alone, some fishermen had to come and give me a hand, which they were more than willing to do when they were about.

I sailed all over, sometimes with Frank, sometimes with Ma and Gran'ma, sometimes alone. As it was, the catboat lasted only that one summer. Things got so tight that Ma said I couldn't have the boat anymore. Mr. Prince said he would have continued to let me use it but things had become tight for him, too, and he had to sell it.

One day Frank started out with "Let's build our own boat. You know all about that bein' as ya gran'pa was a ship builder." Frank often began a project that way, telling me that I knew a lot of stuff that I didn't. But when he said it, I was so proud that he thought so that I couldn't admit not knowing anything.

He knew that I was stupid about boat building, but he also knew that by giving me credit, he had backed me into a corner and that I would do anything to prove him right. Such was a child's ego; so build a boat we would.

What we built was more a raft with a centerboard. We got a mast from Mr. Prince's barn and some old canvas from Mr. Peterson's barn of junk. Frank's ma helped us sew a sail. We sailed all over, soaking wet, and in some ways had more fun with the raft than with all the other boats.

We never had organized sports such as baseball, but we'd go to the island beyond the golf course where there were millions of stones all about the size of ping pong balls, and we'd take sticks and bat the stones for hours. Beyond one wave was a single, two waves was a double, three....Well, you get the idea. It was simple play.

Robert Wolley

Or we'd buy a tennis ball and make up games. Make up. That was simple, I guess, but children don't seem able to make up games any more.

We'd climb the dunes and slide and roll down, just for the pleasure of it. We'd walk the beaches, ten or twelve miles at a stretch, just to see what treasure we could find, and we'd sell what we could to the summer people. They were especially fond of colored glass net floats and large pieces of fish net and hunks of lobster pots. Most of the time we could find enough of that stuff to make the hikes a business.

We'd go to the Coast Guard station to watch the men practicing life saving. In the winter we watched ice cutting. I never remember being bored a day in my life, and when you think of it, we had nothing, no radio, no TV, nothing like that. We never had electricity, ever, until we moved away. But we played card games and board games and read and generally went to bed early so we could get up early and start all over again. Mr. Delanda brought ice every day or two in the summer; I went every day down the street to fetch kerosene for the lamps and stove. It was all just as natural as breathing.

It wasn't simple; it wasn't complicated; it was just the way of it. We were no better or no worse off than others. Life was hard, maybe, but we didn't know any differently, so life was life, not simple or complex or hard or easy; it just was, without pretense or superficialities.

A few years before the war, when so many people started coming to Smalltown, I guess I was impressed by how many summer youths did nothing but sit on the beach all day or play tennis or just tool around in their fancy automobiles. I remember LaSalles mostly because they had that little door just for golf clubs. That stuck with me for years. It was a kind of symbol, I suppose. Later, after the war, I was tempted to buy one from a fellow in Belmont and would have except it ran so badly that I

The Pranks An' Enlightenment of Frank An' Me

didn't dare, but I regret I didn't, even now. I think it might have proved something, but to be honest, I don't know what.

When I was young, everybody looked out for everyone else, not busybodying or snooping but genuine caring. You couldn't walk anywhere without folks noticing. They never asked where you were going, just noted that you went by. But later, if you didn't go by when you came back, well, they noted that, too. Especially, they made such mind notes if you were headed into the Meadows or going to the harbor or the back shore. And it didn't matter if you were a boy or an old woman. Same thing. But it was subtle. They saw you go by; later they asked around if you got home all right. You weren't asked where, exactly, you went or what you did, only if you got back safely.

Many a person was helped by that kind of watching over. Frank and I once, out on the flats trying to walk across the flats to the island, got ourselves stuck in the quicks and couldn't get out. Going deeper and deeper we were. Up to Frank's chest, me most to my waist. We were gone for sure, except old Cap'n Eastman had seen us starting out, and when we didn't come back after a reasonable while, he came looking for us.

It was a good thing he did, too, because it took four men to haul us out.

Rightly so, the men were angry. At the time I thought they were angry because saving us was a big bother, and they were angry at us for all the trouble we caused. Later, I came to realize that they weren't angry *at* us; they were angry *for* us, worried sick that something terrible might have happened to us. That worry, I think, made them angry. Cap'n Eastman must have been mad, too, but all he said was "Reckon you'll be wantin' ta tell ya folks 'bout ya foolishness, won't ya?" He knew some punishment would be handed out. And if it wasn't, he'd know that we didn't tell. And if we didn't tell, he would, because life-taking foolishness wasn't tolerated, not for one second.

Robert Wolley

And, even though we were young, Frank and I knew that we had to have respect for Cap'n Eastman's command because someday we might want to be his crew and because every adult was kind of like a parent, substituting when your own parents weren't around.

There is little of that today, but back then there was. We said "Yes, Ma'am" and "No, Sir" to every adult, treated them with respect, and they treated us no differently than if we were their children, which in a way we were.

Of course, they never struck us or anything like that, although they must have been sorely tempted at times.

This looking out probably was what saved Miss Ella Parsons from dying, she having a peculiar way about herself. Miss Parsons was elderly, way beyond most, although I can't say for sure just how old she was. She was a widow before she was married. By that I mean that her intended husband died just before the wedding. I wasn't even thought of when she was to be married, but from the day I was born, I heard about Ella Parsons and Sam North every time there was a thunder and lightning storm.

It seems that Mr. North — they were going to be married in the Congregational church; it must have been around 1880 or so — decided that the church needed to have its weather vane restored. Apparently the missing weather vane was bronze or brass or copper, no matter, and it had been needed to make cannon for the Civil War. The Congregational church had been a hotbed of abolitionists who decided to donate the weather vane to save the Union and to free the slaves.

Anyway, Mr. North decided for his wedding that the church should have a new weather vane, he being a mariner and no doubt superstitious about anything about the weather. "He wanted ta see fair winds settin' out on the sea o' matrimony," my Gran'ma would say.

The Pranks An' Enlightenment of Frank An' Me

Well, Mr. North must have been a poor mariner. After be had the weather vane made, he was climbing up the church steeple to set the thing in place when he was struck by a bolt of lightning. There were other men on the steeple helping, but the bolt picked just him; nothing happened to the others. Well, that ended Mr. North's wedding plans and got Miss Parsons to wearing black the rest of her life.

It was said that the weather vane was a likeness of Mr. North's packet, but when the lightning got finished with it, it was nowhere to be found, not one little piece of it.

Now, I know that the lightning must have gotten to Miss Parsons, too. I never saw her much, but whenever it was lightning and thundering, Miss Parsons always left her house and walked up to the cemetery where her Sam was resting.

What I say now happened twice that I know, because I remember both times as clear as day.

The Congregational's cemetery was the biggest in town, and when I was young a cart path called Johns Pond Path went to it. Sometime while I was still small, the cart path was pushed on beyond the cemetery to Johns Pond, a tiny pond not more than forty yards across. There used to be only a single lane path from the cemetery to the pond, but someone made a regular path for wagons. At about that time the cemetery got a fence made of granite posts with two pipe rails all around. It wouldn't keep anything in or out, so I never saw the sense of it.

Gran'ma had a widow friend, Mrs. Drew, who lived on the path before you got to the cemetery, so I was familiar with the path and the cemetery and the pond. The pond was home to the biggest turtles I had ever seen.

Anyway, that path was wider and there was the new fence, and one afternoon there was a pretty good lightning storm. Mrs. Drew saw Miss Parsons going to the cemetery as usual, only Miss Parsons didn't return.

Now, the cemetery was up the path, off by itself, and nobody much went to Johns Pond, but Mrs. Drew knew where Miss Parsons was going because Miss Parsons went to the cemetery during every lightning storm.

When Miss Parsons wasn't seen returning after the storm, Mrs. Drew went to find her, and what she found was that the lightning had struck a big oak tree near the fence, that the lightning had jumped from the tree to the fence, splitting every granite post lengthwise, and had laid out the almost — Widow Parsons.

Mrs. Drew was no dumb widow. She could see that Miss Parsons wasn't dead, but she could see also that she wasn't exactly alive. Mrs. Drew couldn't budge old Ella, so, old as she was, she ran all the way to the town hall and called in a fire alarm.

The fire engine came quickly, but when it got to the town hall, there was no fire. Mrs. Drew told the firefighters of course not. She ran all the way into town but sure as thunder she was going to ride back out.

I and the others were in school when all this was happening, but the signal being for the town hall got us out of the school building fast, the school being right next door to the town hall, so everything I tell you after that I saw.

Naturally, with Mrs. Drew up next to the driver, Frank and I and the others chased after the truck. Miss Parsons was sitting up when we got to the cemetery. She wasn't dead, but she was burned on her face. The lightning must have struck her eyeglasses because her face was scarred just as though she had her glasses on. I saw her, and I saw the remarkable splitting of the granite posts.

I told you that this happened twice. A couple of years later, after the cemetery had been protected with new posts, another storm came along and split the posts again, and Miss Parsons was there again. Same ending, too, all burned in the face. And, of

The Pranks An' Enlightenment of Frank An' Me

course, someone saw her going to the cemetery and not coming back and all that. I didn't witness the second time, only the results on Miss Parsons' face.

And for all that, Miss Parsons died in her bed, although my ma and Gran'ma used to argue that she really wanted the lightning to take her to her beloved Samuel North. It was a little joke, I think, that she left a small sum of money to the church and that it was used to repair the fence around the cemetery.

And the church never did get its weather vane. The congregation just stuck a big old spike up on the top of the steeple as a lightning rod with a wire going down to the ground where folks said Mr. North landed dead.

There were always a lot of widows in Smalltown. Some were widows for life, some for only a few weeks. I never did figure out how that all worked in a woman's mind, why some women mourned for fifty years or more, dressed in black from black bonnet to black shoes, and other women wore a black scarf for a month and then got themselves a new husband.

It probably tells you something that I never wondered about the men who got married so soon after their wives passed on. It hardly ever happened that a wife went before her husband, but when it did, no one found it strange that the husband went looking shortly after the funeral.

Perhaps everyone assumed that the man needed looking after and was incapable of taking care of himself, or perhaps it was another unconscious value judgment which made the rules different for men, or maybe women simply could not abide having men who were not married around town.

However that might have been, with so many women and so few men in the town, it was a peculiar mystery that some women got to be married so many times. Take Miss Joy. She was old, too, when I knew her, but she had five husbands, four of them

Robert Wolley

dead by the time I was born, and eighteen children, all moved away long ago.

I remember her at square dances the Legion had in the summer. She'd be dancing away, as old as she was. "Lookin' for number six," Ma would say. "Damn baby factory. Prob'ly have 'nother one when she's ninety." And Ma'd get right angry.

Miss Joy, that was her first husband's name, but everyone called her that, came to Smalltown as a bride, her husband being appointed to the Methodist pulpit. He died a couple of years after, but by then she had had two babies. Then she married up with a Mr. Garnet and had some more babies until he got killed in some kind of accident. Then she married Mr. Pratt, and he drowned, but not before five or six more babies.

And, finally, there was Todd Stone. I knew him some and remember a slew of his children, except I'm not sure which were his and which were hers and which were theirs. Even though she was married to Mr. Stone, everybody still called her Miss Joy. Gran'ma used to make fun of her name, in private of course, although for a long time I didn't understand what Gran'ma meant and found so humorous.

I have memories of Mr. Stone herding a huge fleet of children about in the summer, but none were ever around during school months, and after he died, I don't think I ever saw any of the children again.

Mr. Stone was a generous man and seemed kindly to all the children, even the older ones who were near to going off on their own. If any girl or boy was about when Mr. Stone was buying ice cream for his children, he treated everybody. Lots of summer nights the whole Stone tribe would be on the beach for a picnic. If you were there, too, Mr. Stone came and insisted that you joined their campfire and share the food. And if in the daytime they were playing games, same thing. He included all and everyone. He was well liked.

The Pranks An' Enlightenment of Frank An' Me

Mr. Stone owned an ironworks in Wareham, and a couple of times when things were really bad for us, he gave some Smalltown men work. But when the depression was at its worst, his factory got shut down. I remember that Paul Little was one who worked there. He would come home on weekends. He said that when Mr. Stone called the workers together and told them that the factory was done, he was crying. He asked the men to forgive him because they all were about to lose their jobs. Mr. Little said he believed that Mr. Stone had kept everything going just so the men would have a job.

It was said that Mr. Stone died because he felt so bad. There was gossip about how he died, but I don't know if any of it was true, just as I don't know whether he was one of Smalltown's summer visitors or one of Smalltown's many misplaced natives. His family was one of those that left town during the Civil War, but always there was a Stone house being used by one member of the family or another.

After Mr. Stone died, Miss Joy was gone for a couple of years; when she did return, she came back "ta go huntin'," Ma said. I recall hearing Mr. Prince say once that "Miss Joy'd keep right on givin' joy till she got it right." When I asked him what she was trying to get right, he got all flustered. "What I said ain't for no little boy's wet ears," he said. "It's all in the Bible, 'Be fruitful and multiply'." I made no sense out of that either.

Miss Joy had a few dollars, the inheritance from her late husbands, I suppose, and fixed up the old Stone house. The gardens were especially lovely and were arranged so that people could walk through them and enjoy them without disturbing the people in the house. There was a sign on the gate just off Main Street that had a little poem which I hope I can quote correctly:

> *Flowers mean a lot to me*
> *Because I can share them with thee.*
> *Please walk here and see God's hand*

Robert Wolley

And obey but one command:
If pick a flower you must,
Give it to one you love the most.

Miss Joy never got married again. She traveled a lot, visiting all her children, I suppose. She was a smart-looking woman, even when she was old, and she was a mighty talented piano player. Three or four summers she gave concerts to raise money for the library and a couple of times for the fire department.

And she played in the movie places. That got folks fussing plenty. Smalltown did not have a regular movie house until after every other town, but maybe six or seven times a year, there'd be a movie in the Legion hall or in the basement of the Catholic church, to raise a little money. When I was small, all the movies were silent movies. Everywhere else had talkies, but not Smalltown. Anyway, Miss Joy would play the piano, and boy, just by listening, you could tell what was going on. The few times Ma let me go with Frank, it was exciting just to hear Miss Joy play.

But Miss Joy, being a Methodist, got the Methodist people all riled up, seeing that no respectable Methodist would go to the movies. Work of the devil, they said. There was a lot of talk about Miss Joy giving joy to satan. Then, when talking pictures finally did arrive, what Miss Joy had done was forgotten, I guess, because sometimes she played the organ in the Methodist church for services, and a lot of times she played for funerals.

I got to thinking that do's and don'ts were what appeared right at the time, because I knew that a few Methodist ladies played cards at the Sewing Circle and that a few of the Methodist men sampled a bit of drink, and both were supposed to be dead set against such things.

I remember to this day my first talking picture show. it was filled with knights and farmers and bows and arrows, and I spent

The Pranks An' Enlightenment of Frank An' Me

a lot of time hiding my head because I was plain scared; I spent more time cowering on the floor than watching.

When Smalltown got its movie house, it was built right next door to the Methodist church. Of course I had no hand in all the goings on, but there was some 'ell raised about that. I guess the town meetings for a couple of years were real wars, and Smalltown got as close to a religious war as could be. It was one thing to be a Methodist and to go to a movie, which was bad enough, but to have the House of Satan, as some called it, right next door was terrible. All the noise got quieted down after a while, though. I only went in that movie house once, but once or twice a year Ma would drive us to Sayersville to that movie house.

Smalltown got to be fair size after the turn of the last century. There were two attractions. One was the building of a golf course out on the neck, and the other was the building of a giant, four-story hotel out on the end of a long, long wharf at the end of the Neck. The golf course is still operating.

The hotel, named for a long-ago Indian tribe, came to a sad ending. First, when the depression got bad enough, the hotel scaled down a lot of its operation, and then, toward the middle of the '30s, it shut down altogether. No one could afford to come to Smalltown and make use of it. Then, a year or so later, it burned down to the pilings. That was the biggest fire I had ever seen. No way to put it out, if someone wanted to put it out. I say that because there was considerable speculation about the origin of the fire, many claiming that an insurance recovery was all that was left to the owners. However that might have been, a winter storm finished off what was left. By spring all you could see were a few pilings, with not even the slightest hint of what had been there.

I went to the hotel a couple of times. It wasn't a place that allowed young ones like Frank and me to stroll about. You could, if someone didn't stop you, walk out on the pier and clear around the huge building, but if you got that far, pretty soon someone all dressed up in a fancy uniform would come and ask your name and room number and they would know that you weren't supposed to be there. They would make a lot of noise and fuss about trespassing and kick us off, threatening to have us arrested. Obviously, we didn't look like guests, only ignorant riff-raff, as one man called us. Frank and I paid them no mind and got back at them by ignoring the whole business, just like it wasn't there.

But it was an impressive place, hard to ignore. The first floor had grand eating places and a spectacular ballroom. The second and third floors, I was never on them, were where all the guests stayed, and the fourth floor was where all the servants lived. All summer long at night you could hear a band playing. People used to come from all over the country by train just to live for a week or two at the hotel.

The biggest trouble for Smalltown was that barely a soul ever got to work there; all the help was brought in from off Cape. Offhand, I cannot think of one person from town who had a job there. So, for most of us, it was a novelty. When it went there wasn't too much grieving, except maybe for the loss of tax revenue.

Some of the people, when the depression was over, came back to Smalltown and bought up vacant houses or built their own summer place. And, of course, a few came to Smalltown to live permanently when they retired. In that way the hotel turned out to be good.

Most of the help at the hotel were college students: chamber maids, waiters, cleaning folks, carpenters even. They looked down on everybody from Smalltown because even at our best we were too poor to use the hotel, and hardly anyone in town had ever been near a university. Dr. Hall and the teachers are the

The Pranks An' Enlightenment of Frank An' Me

only ones who come to mind. The hotel had its own medical staff.

I remember that fact well. A few necessary items were brought to the hotel by train, milk being the most obvious item, but everything else was delivered by ship, even ice. The ships came from New Bedford and from Boston every two or three days, and the hotel made a celebration out of their arrivals. The band would play, horns and whistles would blow, and flags and pennants would fly from every conceivable spot.

There was a large mast with a couple of yardarms out on the end of the pier which carried flags all the time, day and night. One entire summer one set of flags broadcast the message, JGIDZ, which in international code said: urgent message, I require immediate assistance. The other yardarm flew ASVEU, meaning: I am undergoing a speed trial; my engines are going full speed astern; I require assistance; bar is dangerous. The EU flags flown together say the latter. I suppose someone took a look at the flags, picked out the ones that appeared most colorful, and made up combinations according to color and design, not realizing the messages being sent.

I don't think anyone would have noticed, either, if it hadn't been for the EU flags. The old sailors got to making fun of the hotel, and then everybody who could started to read the unintentional messages the hotel was sending.

One day one of the supply ships came in, flags flying as usual, with the message screaming out: what a bunch of fancy pants idiots. Even the fishermen went out of their way that day to cruise by the hotel and cheer the supply ship, the captain of the ship greeting every fishing boat with a raised thumb. I suppose not one person in the hotel knew what that as all about.

Pa and Ma went to the hotel to dance once. I asked Ma if she had had a good time. She said it was wonderful, but then I heard her tell Gran'ma that she'd never go back. The people were downright sassy to her and Pa. But Pa wanted to go back, I know, because he talked about the swells forever and ever, how he would be rich one day, and how he'd be one of them.

Maybe he did at that. He bought a fancy coat and hat and some knickers and outlandish socks. Made me laugh, he looked so silly, and Ma was mad again. Pa whacked me for laughing, and Ma whacked me for telling Pa how swell he looked.

Funny, I never use that word, swell, unless I'm thinking about the hotel and the snobs who frequented it and Pa wanting to be one of them.

I suppose they were the same ones who played golf. I wasn't very old when I went to caddy one summer; Frank and I, actually, although Frank went only once. He said that doing nothing was better than that. But I'd go when there was nothing else better. It took nearly an hour to walk to the golf course, unless you could catch a ride, and an hour back, and four or five hours there, so one had to be rather desperate for something to do. The best part was that I was about the only caddy ever. Once in a while a summer boy would try it, but only the poor worked all day for twenty-five or thirty cents.

Fortunately, in those days, the golf bags were light and I could carry two easily, so it wasn't hard work. The worst of it was when some gent wanted to practice hitting balls and I had to run all over creation retrieving them.

The second worst usually was when some gent would hit his ball into places not even rabbits or mice could go. No matter how far into trouble the ball went, they would always expect you to find it, and if you didn't, they'd get extremely angry, as if it was your fault that the ball went wild. Those people hardly ever gave a tip, and if they lost a ball, you could count on getting nothing extra, not even a five-cent soda pop.

I gave up caddying after a couple of years. Golfers were about the rudest and cheapest people I ever met. I didn't need to be treated the way most of them treated me. That wasn't true all the

The Pranks An' Enlightenment of Frank An' Me

time, just mostly, so I retired from a job which I liked but whose people were without manners. I did learn some new ways of taking the Lord's name in vain, though. Better than some of the ways I learned on the boats.

But before I give you the wrong impression, there were summer people who were grand. Some of those people took a real interest in Smalltown and contributed to its life. They supported the churches, helped build the library, bought equipment for the fire department, started an art gallery and a summer theater, donated food and clothing to the poor, and set up scholarship funds. The children always stayed apart from us, but the adults often made close and lasting friendships with Smalltown adults.

I have to mention Dr. Hall. I was going to when I was telling about the hotel, but I got sidetracked. The hotel had its own medical people, so Dr. Hall was never needed there until one day when the supply ship was coming in during a storm. Somehow a lot of people, ten or a dozen, fell or slipped off the pier and were crushed between the ship and the pier. Thank goodness, no one was killed, but the injuries were severe, enough so that that someone pulled the fire alarm. When it was learned that the hotel was on fire, crowds of people rushed to see it. What the firemen found, of course, was a major accident, and the signal went out for medical help. That included Dr. Hall and the Coast Guard.

The Coast Guard would have held an inquiry anyway, but it had trained life-saving people who were needed desperately. Dr. Hall appeared immediately, but when he identified himself, he was refused and none too politely. Even when the Coast Guard first-aid men arrived right after that, they were told they were not needed.

However, when the ship's captain insisted and said that he could be held responsible, the Coast Guardsmen were allowed to tend to some of the injured.

Dr. Hall and a couple of ladies who had been nurses were upset; Dr. Hall was almost in tears. He didn't know what to do. He just stood around, waiting to be allowed to practice his medicine.

Finally, Chief Newfelt came and asked him if the injured could be placed somewhere away from the hotel. The Legion hall was suggested, and the people were moved there eventually. Those who were the most seriously injured would be moved to Barnstable, the nearest town with a hospital.

One of those most badly hurt was a Mr. Brownell. At least I think that was his name. He didn't want to be moved anywhere without a second opinion. It was said that he had a broken back. When he was told that the town had Dr. Hall, he asked to see him. "No one I'd rather have looking after me than a good, old country doctor," he was reported to have said.

Dr. Hall determined that Mr. Brownell did not have a broken back. What he had were some broken ribs, a broken collarbone, and a rupture of the last two or three disks of his spine. It was said that Mr. Brownell shouted "Hot damn!" when told Dr. Hall's opinion, and then he tried to hug the doctor, suffering considerable pain in so doing.

The hotel doctor was furious. It ended up that Chief Newfelt had to separate the doctors and then had to separate the patients, some of whom wanted to be examined by Dr. Hall.

Mr. Brownell was one of those who came back to Smalltown after the depression. In the meantime, he and Dr. Hall became fast friends. It was Mr. Brownell who first started to raise money for a clinic. Unfortunately, both he and Dr. Hall died before that dream was realized.

I don't know when Dr. Hall first came to Smalltown; he used to say he came with the Pilgrims. He was old, a short, somewhat fat man with a head of bushy pure white hair. Why he stayed in Smalltown is beyond me, except he was so loved that perhaps he couldn't disappoint people by leaving. I do remember

The Pranks An' Enlightenment of Frank An' Me

that he made his rounds in a horse-and-buggy when I was small; later he got a Ford like Pa's. I never remember Dr. Hall without his doctor's bag, a small black thing filled with medicine and stuff, some of the stuff pieces of candy and tiny toys for us children.

When I was six, I was sick near to death. To this day I don't know what I had, but I was sick all summer. For a long while Dr. Hall came every day. He made me take some orange pills that nearly burned out my throat and stomach. But what I remember most is that when I was first taken sick, he stayed with me and Ma for several days and nights. Gran'ma moved in with Ma, and Dr. Hall used Gran'ma's bed. I was a whole year recovering from that mysterious illness.

Then I remember having terrible earaches when I was about thirteen. Dr. Hall operated on me right in Ma's bed. Cut my ear open and let out a lot of pus. I fought the ether when he put one of Ma's strainers over my mouth and nose. Lordy, that was horrible stuff; it burned something awful and made me sick for a couple of days after. For many days while I was getting better, Dr. Hall would come and look me over and then stay and play games with me for a time. I never forgot that extra kindness.

He treated everybody like that. I wish that I could have told him later, when he was dying, what he had meant to me, but I was not in Smalltown. I'm sure that many people took the time to treat him as he had treated us. He was a doctor to the soul and heart as well as to the body.

Nobody died without Dr. Hall being there to ease their way out of this world; nobody stayed sick for lack of money; nobody lived in Smalltown for long without offering a prayer of thanksgiving to the Lord for His having given us Dr. Hall.

Once I did tell Dr. Hall what he meant to me, albeit quite unintentionally. I told him that when I was a youngster, I thought God might look like him, only somewhat taller and a wee bit thinner. Dr. Hall was held in such regard that I don't think God would have minded the comparison.

Dr. Hall's reaction was memorable. "Well," he said, "if God looks like me, he sure is a poor specimen. I can't imagine what God looks like, probably all of us rolled up into one magnificent figure: white, black, tall, short, thin, fat, blue-eyed, brown-eyed; he'd have bushy brown hair and no hair and white hair. He'd laugh at your thought, not to be mean but to express the thought that everyone looks like God. We are all God's children. I thank you for the honor, but you know, I think God must look like you." That was Dr. Hall.

When Gran'ma was dying from cancer, Dr. Hall was Ma's salvation. He treated Ma for her own depression and nervousness just as he treated Gran'ma for her endless pain. He was a country doctor, never claimed even that, yet he was one of the threads that held our world together.

The Pranks An' Enlightenment of Frank An' Me

Chapter VII

When Frank an' Me Were Men

Robert Wolley

Since pirate ships are associated with the Cape, it's sometimes asked if there ever were any slave ships out of Smalltown before the Civil War. I don't know of any that were fitted out to carry slaves from Africa; I don't even know of any Smalltown man that sailed on a slave ship, but since Cape men sailed all over the world in all kinds of vessels, there might have been some. I never heard any man own up to it, either for himself or for his ancestors.

Nobody would have admitted to it if it had been true. I think Smalltown had no sympathy for slavery. At least Smalltown was for the North in the Civil War and sent more than her share to fight, both on land and sea.

I would say that Smalltown had a conscience and thought about happenings elsewhere, to some degree at least. We were off on the end of the world here, with little say in what went on, but we worried, and surely before my time others worried about things such as markets and money and jobs and wars. Packet owners worried about the railroad, fishermen worried about Canadian fishermen, lumbermen worried about the supply of lumber, people worried about themselves and about each other.

And some people worried about injustice and poverty and equality. I didn't have such worries when I was young because I didn't know any better, although I began to come of age when I was twelve and thirteen. I'll tell you something you will never read in any other book.

"Now ya ain't got the right of it." That was old Bill's final word; nothing more'd be said, and we knew it. But that day it gnawed at us something awful.

Old Bill was about the only fisherman who ever took the time to jaw regularly with us, we being young and mostly a nuisance and underfoot. But when Bill said no or stop or shut up, we did. Old Bill wasn't too much older than Frank and I; he looked old, that's for sure, all sunburnt and unshaven usually and

The Pranks An' Enlightenment of Frank An' Me

wrapped up tightly in his fisherman's rags, even in summer. He was only thirteen or fifteen years before us.

Now we're on his boat and scared for our lives because Bill is into something dark and fearsome.

But I'd better back up a bit. Living alone as he did, Bill suddenly gave up his shack behind our house and started building a grand new house down on the harbor. Not long after it was finished, he disappeared for a time.

That's when our problem came. He and we shared a water tower, his invention, but when he went, he took the pump and engine. We had no water. We had a hand pump, but the well was so deep that we pumped nothing but air. So we had trouble, mostly mine, because it was just Ma and Gran'ma and me, Pa having left, and I had to carry water from Cole's Inn all day long.

We fussed over the water matter a whole lot, but no one cared much because of the mystery of Bill's leaving and coming back, when finally he did come back.

It seems he went off with Cap'n Joyce on the captain's cod boat. When the *Missus* came home, Cap'n Joyce was not on board. In his place, Bill had a beautiful woman. People said he anchored the Missus opposite his new house, rowed the longboat ashore, paraded the lady up the beach to his house, and said not a word to anyone. The lady was seldom seen for a good long while, and when she was, she was growing fatter in the belly.

Frank and I did see her a couple of times because, during our twelfth summer, we sometimes worked for Bill when he went day-hauling cod or mackerel or squid. Between us, we did a man's work. Frank and I would stop at Bill's house to see if he could use us on the boat or to collect wages. We'd see Bill's lady; nice she was, and free with cookies and milk, and pretty. Lordy, was she pretty! Bill about walked on his knees for her and was shaving and dressing neatly.

Robert Wolley

We never went to his house more than six times after she came, but she was getting fat. Frank said his ma said she was fragrant or something like that.

We got to speculating about that. We didn't know much about babies or how they got started. We had some ideas, but mostly we were ignorant. Of course, we knew some physical differences. Twice that summer we crawled the dunes to watch the summer girls sun on the beach and swim in the ocean without anything on. We noted certain things, but what amused us the most was how the girls held their breasts when they ran, and we noted certain other differences. But in those days the excitement was in the peeking, far more than what we saw.

About the same time that Bill's wife was growing her baby, folks were in a tizzie about Cap'n Joyce, especially his wife. For a time we hadn't seen that old lady, nor had Gran'ma, she being Mrs. Joyce's friend.

But one day, about the time Bill's wife had her baby, Mrs. Joyce walked up town, all dressed in black. Gran'ma said she was a widow, wearing black because the captain had gone and gotten himself killed.

Early the next spring, Bill sold his boat and started using the Missus exclusively. Right after that, the day school was over for the summer, Bill came to the house. Ma lit into him about the water tower and the pump. She must have been storing up a lot of madness because she yelled at Bill and ended up pushing him around the yard.

When she stopped, Bill said that he would put back the pump and engine; it would cost Ma twenty-five dollars. Ma started to argue about the price but Bill reminded her that he built the tower and owned everything and had only tied us in as a favor. That quieted Ma some. And then Bill said he would take the money from my wages.

What wages, yelled Ma? And that's when it really started. One man could run the Missus, but it took at least three to fish

The Pranks An' Enlightenment of Frank An' Me

her. I didn't know at that moment that no one would go fishing with Bill. He needed a couple of men but would settle for Frank and me.

Never, said Ma, not even if we starved, and she started blaming Bill for Cap'n Joyce's dying, lit into him real good, saying he had had a hand in making Mrs. Joyce a widow. The whole town was of the opinion that Bill was a murderer.

Bill made no answer to Ma's tirade. Ma said I couldn't ever fish with Bill again, he being such a low-down creature and all. I guess Frank's parents were of the same mind because Frank didn't set foot on the Missus either.

With no crew, the Missus just swung on her mooring line, never going for cod or mackerel or squid. Bill's lady had had her child; there were diapers on the back line, but I never saw her, not being allowed to go to Bill's house.

Folks began to say awful things about Bill and Cap'n Joyce. Bill never fished, but he kept his house up with fresh paint and flowers. That set the tongues to wagging, and no one was worse at it than Ma. Not only had she convicted Bill of doing in Cap'n Joyce, well, maybe not that but close to it; she convicted him of some mighty unlawful doings. No one in the town would give him the time of day. It seemed as if no one would even recognize him; he couldn't even buy anything in the stores or gas for the boat. Yet that didn't seem to matter too much to Bill. Whenever he came ashore, his longboat was always full. And he must have been getting gas somewhere.

Toward the end of June the Missus was absent from the harbor for a long spell. Frank and I figured Bill had sold her, but one morning when I was cutting bait in Charlie Radar's shack, in came the Missus, Bill at the helm, with a load of summer people, all just as big as life, and for the whole month of July, every few days, the Missus would disappear for two or three days at a stretch.

Robert Wolley

Frank and I were the same age; our birthdays were within two weeks of each other's. Frank was the older, so I got to calling him Old Frank. When we were within hearing of the summer girls, he liked that.

At the end of July, on my birthday, I told Ma I was going fishing full-time. Lordy, what a fuss she raised, all about school and being a baby and her needing me around the house. School was the least of my concern. School closed and reopened depending on the season and the fishing and at times on the extent of wild cranberry and beach plum harvests. Those were important cash crops. School closed in the fall for them and if there was a good mackerel run; closed in late winter when the cod were good; closed in the spring for mackerel and squid.

Even when Frank and I were in school during those later years, there were just six students, counting the Chambers kids, all girls who came like peas out of a pod one right after the other, all four being only about three years apart. Ma said that Mrs. Chambers spent her whole life on her back, but at the time I didn't know what that was supposed to have meant. Mrs. Chambers certainly must have worked hard, the girls all dressed neat and proper in their homemade dresses.

Those were hard years, and ma gave in, not to full-time fishing but to more of it. Maybe she talked with Frank's parents because one day we were discussing it and the whole idea seemed settled. The trouble was, no one wanted two boys. We took away a man's wages, they said. So finally we ended up in front of Bill's house.

I remember that day for sure. He and his wife were having a terrible fight. She was screaming about the child not growing up with friends. We were about to take off when Bill came bolting through the front door.

He asked us what we wanted. Frank thought he was going to hit us. When I told him we wanted to work on the Missus, he laughed. Then he looked me squarely in the eyes and asked if my

The Pranks An' Enlightenment of Frank An' Me

ma knew what I was doing. Right off I looked him in the eyes and answered yes. It was partly true. She knew I was looking to join a boat. She didn't know that I was asking Bill. The fact was, she'd have skinned me if she knew I was even talking with him.

He quieted down and said he'd think about it. We could stand by the longboat at five the next morning. If he decided to take us on, we'd go with him. If not, he would give us an hour's pay just for showing up.

I didn't tell Ma, just got up the next morning and waited on the beach with Frank. When Bill came he didn't say anything, just pointed to the longboat. We jumped in eagerly, and Bill rowed us to the Missus.

Frank and I had never been on the Missus, so once Bill got the engine started and dropped the mooring and headed out, we went exploring. There was nothing special about the boat other than she was bigger than most. The only unusual thing we noticed was how little she smelled of fish, as though she had been cleaned up and not used for fishing at all.

We made coffee the way Bill had taught us before, and sandwiches for later on, and then went looking for our fishing gear, figuring maybe we'd be handlining for deep cod or maybe longlining for tuna. Finding no fishing gear at all, we went to the wheelhouse to ask Bill what for.

No fishing this trip, he said. "Going to meet somebody and take on a cargo." That didn't mean anything to me, but Frank got all upset and said something about listening to his pa. That didn't make any sense to me either. He and Bill got to yelling and carrying on. Frank yelled something about it all being true. Bill yelled it wasn't.

I had no idea what the yelling was all about, so when Frank stomped out of the wheelhouse, I followed. His pa, Frank said, said Bill and Cap'n Joyce had gotten into the rackets. I didn't know what that meant. Frank said that Bill and Cap'n Joyce must have been running rum. I knew what that meant, Ma being a Methodist forever at war against the devil and the devil's rum being one of those catches that regularly came ashore at night and, of course, having my own pa doing the devil's own work right there between the beach and the Harris farm. Oh yes, I knew well what rumrunning was.

So, Frank went on, Bill must have swindled Cap'n Joyce out of his boat, did him in, and got the rumrunning trade all to himself, and, in Frank's pa's eyes, Bill's woman was a payoff, a sinful reward for doing the devil's business, a reward given to Bill by the devil himself. And, said Frank, we weren't safe because now we knew that Bill would do us in.

Lord Almighty was I scared, because if Bill didn't get me, the devil would, and if Bill and the devil didn't get me, my own ma and the Lord Himself would punish me eternally. I could see 'ell just waiting for me.

What I couldn't see was a way of escaping. We had been going for hours, straight out to sea. I wanted to cry, me being only thirteen and a fatherless child, but about then the engine shut down and Bill was hollering for us. Better go, said Frank. He being older, I let him be the boss.

Bill gave us a frightful look and wanted to know what we had been up to. Right off I blurted out about him doing in Cap'n Joyce and making Mrs. Joyce a widow. And running rum.

That's when Bill said we didn't have the right of it. But he wouldn't say anything more. Lord, I had a pain in my belly, and I had to go to the head something awful. I expected that Frank felt the same way. I excused myself and went to do my necessary. Bill said nothing. I waited for Frank but he didn't come, so finally I went back to the wheelhouse. Frank wasn't there!

"Ya done him in," I yelled. Bill got all red in the face. He pointed to the bow. Frank was hankered down against the bulwark, not a good place to be if you were feeling poorly. Bill had started the engine again and was moving the boat slowly against the mild chop. Even so, the bow pitched up and down.

The Pranks An' Enlightenment of Frank An' Me

After a while, Bill got the boat moving at a better clip, smoothing it out but taking us farther from home. We were about five hours from Smalltown.

Another hour and then Bill shut the engine down again. "Boys," he yelled, "get your miserable tails up here." There was nothing but to do what he said.

"Boys," he spoke very softly, "you're a sorry mess, a poor s'cuse for human bein's. But I guess it ain't your fault. Anyway, I got some 'plainin' ta do, I reckon. Your parents could of 'plained, but they be too blind to see the truth an' too ready ta jump ta conclusions.

"First, 'bout Cap'n Joyce, since you're goin' ta see him soon. He ain't dead. Nor did he leave Mrs. Joyce. She kicked him out of his own house 'cause she took up with Jonathan Burger, that there evangelist up in Northam. Said she got religion, but what she got was caught in bed with the reverend. So the Cap'n got out; said he'd end up killin' the both of 'em if he didn't. His woman knowed that."

Lord Almighty, I was hearing things I never had heard. But was it true? And how come Ma and Gran'ma didn't know? Or did they know and keep it secret? But I didn't have time for speculation. Bill kept going.

"But when Burger up an' died, jest like that, an' the poor woman's left high an' dry, she took to wearin' the black. Folks saw her an' wanted ta believe the black were for the Cap'n, but the black really was for that so-called preacher man of God."

Was that true? My education was sure being expanded.

"I bought the Missus from the Cap'n 'cause he couldn't stand the boat, seein' how he named it for his wife. The Cap'n wants me ta change her name, but I ain't got a better one yet."

Well, Bill sounded truthful. I looked at Frank; he was just plain dumb, his mouth open and eyes bugging out. But what we had heard was just the beginning. Bill let all that sink in for a couple of minutes.

Robert Wolley

"Now, I know what people say 'bout my wife. We're married legal an' proper. An' she ain't no prize that I won, 'though she be a prize, a true an' wonderful woman. She be the Cap'n's daughter. An' we married with the Cap'n's blessin'."

That was a stopper. I knew now that Bill was leading us on with lies because the Widow Joyce was known for not having any children, living or dead. Barren, my Gran'ma used to say.

I looked at Frank again. His expression hadn't changed. He just looked at Bill with a stupid, blank stare. If he had any thoughts, none came through. Maybe there wasn't time because Bill kept right on going.

"Cap'n Joyce had two wives. The wife we knowed was number two. Him an' the first wife had a daughter; lived all her twenty-three years with the Cap'n's parents 'bove Boston. Her ma died givin' birth ta her. That was at sea somewhere 'tween Europe an' America.

"The Cap'n being at sea mostly had ta have a home for the girl. When the Cap'n settled in Smalltown an' took Mrs. Joyce for his wife, she wouldn't take the child. That was 'bout twenty years 'go. So the Cap'n left his daughter with his parents, but he visited her 'most every quarter o' the moon an' sent her money, an' that was one reason why the Cap'n took ta fishin' 'stead of makin' them long hauls ta South America an' Europe, sellin' an' tradin'."

Lordy, I was learning a lot, but I couldn't say a word. I didn't know what to say. Actually, I thought that Cap'n Joyce had been in Smalltown forever. He was a very private person and seldom spoke unless asked a direct question. He always kept to himself, as did Mrs. Joyce, although I did know that her family had lived in Smalltown for a couple of generations. Her parents both died when she was young but of age, and I guess I remember hearing that she kept their house, albeit alone, and that was the house where she and Cap'n Joyce lived. It popped into my mind that the Cap'n's crew, except sometimes for Bill, came from

The Pranks An' Enlightenment of Frank An' Me

somewhere else. But that was common in Smalltown; there were few men who wanted to crew, most owning their own boats.

While I was having those thoughts, Bill just kept on talking. It seems that when Bill and the Cap'n left Smalltown the summer before, it was so that the Cap'n could live with his daughter and his parents for a spell. The parents were getting old and needed some looking after. Cap'n Joyce intended to sell the Missus; he had taken on a job as a tugboat captain in Boston harbor.

Now, Bill was saying, he used to go with the Cap'n sometimes when he visited his daughter, and Bill and her got in love. Bill even fixed it in his head to marry her, even built that new house. No one told the Cap'n, though.

Anyway, when the Cap'n was fixing to leave, he asked Bill to help him, not knowing what was in Bill's mind. When he saw Bill and his daughter mooning together, he put it all together and said he would sell the Missus to Bill so he would have a proper boat for a proper living. Everything was fine except for the speculation and the gossip. Everyone stood against them, not knowing the right of it.

Being ignorant, I didn't know what was the truth. Bill surely sounded truthful.

"But," asked Frank, the first time he'd said anything since Bill started talking, "what are we doin' in the middle o' the ocean?"

"Ain't in the middle o' the ocean," said Bill. "If ya had been payin' 'tention, ya'd know that we're 'bout thirteen miles out an' we're goin' ta meet Cap'n Joyce, take a little cargo from 'im."

"I knowed it! Rum!"

"Not this trip," grinned Bill, "we ain't, though I been knowed ta find a couple of bottles."

"What then?" I asked.

"People, families wantin' ta work, families starvin', families that have come some consid'rable distance ta America."

"Where from?"

Robert Wolley

"Most of 'em come from 'round New York or down from Canada, havin' got there from Cuba an' Ireland, from Russia an' Poland an' the islands of Europe. Not the sick ones; Cap'n Joyce won't take that bunch, but the ones with no families in the U.S. of A. or no job or money. He gets 'em after others picks 'em up in Maine an' Nova Scotia or down 'long Long Island or other places where they's been hiding."

Bill waited a minute for that to sink in, but he was talking over our heads. That didn't matter to him; he just continued. "Course there's them that helps all this, them that gives them people ta the Cap'n an' them the Cap'n gives 'em ta, some like me up an' down the coast, an' I delivers 'em ta those who wait."

I had a parcel of questions: how did Bill get started doing this, how long has he been doing it, did he use his own boat before getting the Missus, were there others from Smalltown doing the same thing?

Instead, I asked the dumbest question of all, "If them people ain't got no money, how ya get paid?"

Bill didn't give much of an answer. "I gets paid," is all he said.

Later, I found out that a lot of people, some who cruised on the Missus in the summer, organized in what they called "societies," in what Bill called "a network," paid Bill and the Cap'n and others because they wanted people to have a chance in this country. Of course I didn't know anything like that then, didn't know what quotas were and really didn't understand the full implication of the word "immigrant." I don't believe that I fully appreciated that one couldn't just come to America.

And until I saw those families and children, I didn't really know what poor or starving was. We were poor, but we never starved. We didn't have much, but we always had food.

About twenty miles off Plymouth and about fourteen miles north of Race Point, well outside the limit of the federal boats, we met Cap'n Joyce. Cap'n Joyce set three families on the Missus

The Pranks An' Enlightenment of Frank An' Me

from among the bunch of families he had on board a converted schooner.

After the Cap'n talked with Bill, he came to Frank and me and shook our hands, treating us like grown men, and thanked us. I don't think I ever talked with the Cap'n in my whole life, but he wanted Frank and me to talk about the village and the people. He even asked about Mrs. Joyce. When we said goodbye, he thanked us again, and, pointing to the children, said he hoped they could have a chance to grow up as good as Frank and me. That was the last time we ever saw him.

Bill was troubled to get away. That's when he told us we were going against the law, smuggling people. I used to hear about pirates and Frank and I played some at being pirates, but Bill said this was no game, telling us something about Smalltown folks running past Confederate gunships and saving slaves during the Civil War, about Smalltown sailors slipping the British before that. He said Cap'n Joyce had been doing stuff like that half his life, ever since he sailed to the Spanish isles once. His first wife was one he snitched from the government somewhere, along with her family. Bill didn't make it clear which government Cap'n Joyce had fooled, American or Spanish. It didn't matter; the story was exciting as it was. Cap'n Joyce took that family to a landing near Boston and asked the daughter to sail with him, which she did until she died in childbirth. So maybe she wasn't his legal wife. I didn't ask. And maybe that gave Mrs. Joyce some leverage when she refused to accept the child. I couldn't fathom it, nor, I confess now, did I try terribly hard.

We listened to Bill, but I can't say that we understood all that he was saying. But when he called us good men and how we were plumb in the mold of Smalltown men, we felt proud. We didn't realize then the serious fuss we were in or that there was a real possibility of being shot at and arrested and, worst, killed.

We moved slowly, not making much headway, until toward sunset when Bill headed to shore. We landed in three different places, being met each time by some men, and letting a family off at each landing. Frank and I played some with the children even if we couldn't understand a word they said, but mostly we fed them, and their parents, too.

We got home just before sun-up. Bill gave each of us ten dollars, more money than I'd ever seen in my hand at one time, and told us we had done well.

Ma was sleeping right by the door in a straight chair. I did my best to slide on by, but I woke her. She was fit to be tied and started screaming even before she was awake. She knew I had been with Bill because every other boat was in the harbor. She whacked me across the head, and when I turned away, she kicked my south side. Before I could run out, she had me by the ear, shaking my head something fearful. Then out the door and straight up the hill toward the Methodist parsonage, and at 5:30 in the morning, she was pounding on the Reverend Ellsworth's door with all her fury.

The parson finally answered. I could see his nightshirt under his pants. Ma was explaining, but she was going too fast for the preacher. When Mrs. Ellsworth came downstairs, she quieted Ma some. Breakfast, she said, would help. I wasn't hungry in the least, but anything might help. Ma let go of my aching ear.

Mr. Ellsworth took me into his office, study, I think he called it. I told him everything, leaving nothing out, including the devil himself.

"Yes, yes," he said. "I see. Hum. Hum. Such business." Things like that. At least he didn't get mad.

In fact, things were going pretty well between the reverend and me until Bill showed up with his wife and child.

"Cap'n Joyce is dead," Bill announced. Gov'ment boat found 'em an' sank 'em. All dead, the cap'n, crew, whole families." Bill was mad, but his wife was crying, the cap'n being her father and all. It seems the news came over the radio.

The Pranks An' Enlightenment of Frank An' Me

Mr. Ellsworth tried to comfort Bill's wife, and the women all hugged, and Mrs. Ellsworth led Ma and Bill's wife into the sitting room. Mr. Ellsworth took Bill's hand.

"It's all over," he said, "for now anyway. I'm sorry 'bout Cap'n Joyce. He was doing the Lord's work." Then he added, "We're ready to move you if you want to go. Today, if you want."

Bill shook his head no. I wasn't too bright maybe, but I could tell that they were all in it together, the preacher, the Cap'n, Bill, and a lot of others. Later I would know that several from Smalltown, including some who seemed to ignore and shut Bill and his wife out, were taking part. And later I would know that much of the shunning of Bill and his family was a deliberate act to protect everybody concerned.

Right in the middle of all this, Mr. Ellsworth laughed. "Now," he shouted out, "the widow's got a right to wear her black." Even Bill laughed, although he allowed that that was a terrible thing for a preaching man to say.

"Indeed. I should apologize, and I will in my prayers. But remember this, in another time the lady in question would have been branded or stoned."

"Or both," added Bill.

"Exactly." Mr. Ellsworth was silent for a couple of minutes. "This may not be the time for it, but I have to admonish you for risking two young boys, not only putting their lives at risk but for involving them in something for which they are too young and of which their parents might disapprove most strongly."

"I'm not makin' 'cuses, Reverend, but right up to five-thirty yesterday morning I were hopin' for someone else, but no one came. I had no way to contact the cap'n; he had already sailed. You know well 'nough that at least one person has to help with them families. I had to take the boys. It was as simple as that. Or not go, an' that would have been worse. I made the choice 'cause I had no choice."

Robert Wolley

Mr. Ellsworth nodded in agreement.

Most of the bodies, including Cap'n Joyce were recovered by the next day. The captain's was returned to Smalltown. I don't know where the others went.

When the captain was buried, Mr. Ellsworth spoke for nearly an hour about hopes and dreams and opportunities, about the Lord's sacrifice and the captain's and others', about God wanting his children to serve others, about the devil's tools of suspicion and gossip. He even got in a word about something called "fronication." Frank and I couldn't make head or tail about that except you ought not do it, whatever it was.

A lot of summer folks came to the funeral, and folks I had never seen before. Even some of the summer girls came with their parents. Frank and I watched them and winked at each other because a few of them we had seen from the dunes. About the only one who didn't attend was the captain's widow.

Mrs. Joyce lived a long time, long after Frank and I learned why we enjoyed peeking at the summer girls, long after we knew what fornication was, long after we partnered a fishing boat, long after Frank and Gran'ma went, and long after Bill's daughter grew up and went off to college, the first ever from our town to go. It would have made the captain proud, she being his granddaughter and all.

The Pranks An' Enlightenment of Frank An' Me

Chapter VIII

Between Bein' Child an' Man

Robert Wolley

Once, a man accused me of surrealism. I didn't know what he meant. He assured me that he meant no negative criticism, only that sometimes I brought out ideas in very unusual ways. I thought that sounded negative. He explained that when I was growing up, big things were happening in this country. In 1920, the 17th Amendment to the Constitution was passed, stopping the sale and drinking of liquor. In the 1920s, Congress passed immigration restriction acts. He said I was telling about those things when really I was only telling about myself. Yet, through the stories, I was telling something about history.

I could see that. There is nothing that we do that is not connected somehow to other people and other places.

Then he went on to say that my little pieces of history, from my viewpoint, were the whole event, when, of course, they were not. I could see that, too.

When I told about knocking down poles in the Meadows, the man said, and making my father lose his way when he was moving illegal liquor, might seem to have nothing to do with mass murder in Chicago, but it did. What Frank and I did and the killings that took place in Chicago because of Prohibition were connected. Smalltown and Ellis Island in New York harbor were connected because of the Johnson Acts limiting immigration.

I hadn't thought about all that in such intimate terms, hadn't thought about it at all at the time, but Smalltown was connected to the world, even when we didn't realize it.

The 1920s were called the "lost generation" decade. It was claimed that America was all done, that what used to be called "the Puritan ethic," hard work and resisting temptations, was all wrong, that morals of all kinds were old-fashioned, that anybody who thought for himself probably was evil. A whole bunch of stuff like that. Places like Smalltown were written off as having

The Pranks An' Enlightenment of Frank An' Me

no energy or vitality or purpose, as places of quiet desperation in which people mostly did a lot of bad things to each other.

A long time ago I came to resent that description. Desperate we were mostly to make ends meet. Parents were desperate to make something better for their children. But we had energy. Lord, we would have worked at anything and for anything. We preserved the so-called Puritan ethics even if they were called that only because they were supposed to relate back to the Pilgrims and Puritans. We were not lazy, nor did we do bad things to each other, nor did we ever forget right from wrong. Oh, there were wrong things done and now and then bad, terrible things done, single things, and when they were done, we knew right from wrong and did our best to correct them.

I want to tell you about three men. Up in the Methodist church was Mr. Ellsworth, a true man of God. But there was no one harder working or more caring than Mr. Evans in the Congregationalist church or Father Costa when he came to the Catholic church. Those men pastored in the town all the years I was growing up without asking once who was of what church. No one was ever sick or injured or in need that had to look beyond one of those men. And if you were of no faith, it made no difference.

Only once was there a public argument among them, and that was when some men came to Smalltown to organize for the KKK. The Catholic church was the target for abuse, the church having some black folks and some with Indian blood and many people of mixed Portuguese and Negro and Indian blood.

That was a terrible few weeks for Smalltown. I don't remember the exact year; I guess it was in the late '20s or early '30s because that was when the KKK had a big revival and spread up from the South, not only to peddle hate against the blacks but against the Jews and Catholics and the whites who were friendly

Robert Wolley

or in business with Jews and Catholics or blacks, although there were no Jews in Smalltown that I knew of.

But if I don't remember the exact year, I do remember most of the bits and pieces of it.

Most of the Portuguese, Africans, Indians, and those "mixed" went to the Catholic church. Some of everything went to all three church, but I think most of those I named were Catholic.

I wasn't too old. I never heard what the KKK men said, only that the most upset were Father Costa and the Catholics, Frank's ma and pa among them, and Aunt Hattie. I remember her telling Gran'ma what an evil thing had come to town.

One Sunday, because of something that happened but which I can't recall, Father Costa stood right out on Main Street in front of his church just after the other churches let out from their services, so it must have been just after noon, and preached against the KKK.

That Father Costa would do that was unthinkable. He was not a daily public figure on Main Street, not like the two ministers. And he never projected himself into the daily affairs of the town, never had a cup of coffee in the newsstore even.

Beyond the fact of his preaching in public, the only thing I remember is that he said that if the Reverends Evans and Ellsworth didn't join him in resisting the devil, they were of the anti-christ.

Maybe thirty people heard Father Costa that noon. Within minutes, two hundred people knew what he had said. It was a remarkable day. Later, after I knew a lot more than I did then, I realized just how strong the words were, considering that a lot of Protestant churches openly supported the Klan in those days. And surprisingly, given the religious climate of the day, that any Catholic priest would call on Protestant clergymen for help. Father Costa's action speaks to the seriousness of the threat.

Below the surface there were deep prejudices. There were wonderful individual Catholics worshipping in strange, meaning different, ways, but there was always the threat of popery and who knew what else. In Smalltown WASPs were not the majority, but they were the power.

The KKK presence brought some of the prejudice to the surface and exposed a raw nerve. And once exposed, people had to face up to the fact. Father Costa had forced the issue; there was no way to avoid it.

For a time I think that all the pastors did was say that the KKK couldn't use their churches, if they ever did, which I don't know. But that did nothing. The KKK used the Legion hall for a few meetings, but some of the Legionnaires were Catholic and some weren't all white, so that didn't last long, but it did upset a few, both the meetings in the hall and the closing of the hall to more meetings. Sides were being drawn.

I don't know how many Klansmen were in Smalltown, five or six. I never saw them much. They passed out papers and talked with folks, mostly men. They wanted to talk to the school children but didn't. They were in town for weeks on end and stirred things up a bit. They didn't stay in Smalltown at night, just rode into town each day in their two big cars at about the time town hall opened for business.

At the end of June they announced a big rally and free food and fireworks for the Fourth of July. Smalltown always made a big day out of the Fourth on the town beach, with games and food and a band that came from Sayersville, and at night there was a huge bonfire and singing and speeches. The main speech just before the bonfire was lit was always given by one of the school children. Frank gave it once.

That year the speech was to be given by Asturia Chambers. Mrs. Chambers was Portuguese, and she and the girls were Catholic. The KKK men made it known that they didn't like that, the Fourth of July being, they said, for Americans, the pure, white, non-Catholic/non-Jew kind.

Robert Wolley

So, the KKK was going to have its own rally at the other end of the beach. People were wagering on which affair would get the bigger crowd.

There was a man named "Kitts" David who ran a nice boat and who came to the harbor each year from down Maine. He would come at the end of June with his fishing crew and fish for two or three weeks for horse mackerel and then follow them up the coast to the Gulf of Maine.

Mr. David was a big man, all shiny-black. He was born in the West Indies. His crew was black, too. In those days no one wanted the horse mackerel; they wrecked nets and the weirs something fearful. Fisherman hated them. Now they are called school tuna, and they're a valuable catch. Regretfully, they have been so over-fished that they're seldom seen, but back to the time I'm talking about they were considered by Cape fishermen as worthless and trouble. So Kitts David was doing our fishermen a favor by taking them. He always paid his bills for gas and food and was always welcome.

He never fished on Sundays. He and his crew always went to the Mother of our Savior church, and every year Father Costa blessed his ship the first Sunday Mr. David was in town.

The night before the Fourth, the *Regina*, that was Mr. David's boat, exploded, and Mr. David and his crew of five were killed.

It could have been an accident. Sometimes those things happened, but apparently one of the KKK men said to someone that accidents like that were how to take care of people like Mr. David. So maybe the Klan blew up the Regina. I don't think it ever was proved, but by midday everybody had taken sides.

It wasn't like any Fourth of July I had ever known. If the KKK man hadn't said anything, perhaps nothing would have happened.

The Pranks An' Enlightenment of Frank An' Me

First, the Fourth of July activities planned by the town were called off, but at supper, Gran'ma said she was going to help Father Costa and the Catholics down at the beach. The KKK hadn't called off its rally and apparently Father Costa was going to confront them. Ma said she would go, too.

Ma told me I couldn't go, being too young and not knowing anything. So, naturally, as soon as Ma and Gran'ma went out the door, so did I.

And so must have Father Costa and part of his congregation. Down on the beach I saw Miss Harper and Aunt Hattie and Mr. Prince and others standing with Father Costa and his flock.

On the other end of the beach were the KKK men wearing funny white-pointed hats and white coveralls. With them were some of Smalltown's World War I men and some men I had never seen before. It looked as if they were prepared for a fight.

The two groups just stared at each other for a time, but after a while Father Costa started leading about fifty people along the beach, Father Costa carrying a great big cross. Walking in the sand wasn't too easy because it was dry and soft, so the whole of Father Costa's bunch seemed to plod along in slow motion but all the time moving toward the Klan and the others.

The KKK men had planted a gigantic cross in the sand, and when Father Costa got about sixty, seventy yards away, they lit it on fire. Lordy, did it blaze, and it must have been hot because the men moved off to the side. That's when I saw something else. Two of the men in the white hats and coveralls had guns hidden in their clothing, shotguns like Pa and Cloyd used to use.

I remember thinking that the event was not entertainment and wishing that none of the people were there, fifty people moving toward fifteen or twenty and another large group of people watching like me. One of our teachers told us once that when armies fought, even up to the Civil War, a favorite pastime was for people to drive to the battleground, have a picnic, and watch the fighting. That's what I was doing, and other spectators were spread out along the beach waiting for whatever action was going to occur.

To me the guns made the KKK look like an army, their hats swaying in time with the plodding steps coming toward them.

When one of the Klan lifted up his shotgun, I remember standing up from where I was hiding and yelling. I don't remember what I yelled, something about guns, I suppose. Nobody heard me because at that moment Mr. Peterson and his funeral wagon charged into the middle of the confrontation. Never before had I seen Mr. Peterson's wagon hauled by more than one horse, but this time he had four, and they charged hell-bent-for-leather down the beach, sand flying, and right between the two sides. And when he stopped the wagon, out got Dr. Hall, Mr. Beers, Mr. Ellsworth, and Mr. Evans.

The two ministers went to Father Costa and hugged him. Dr. Hall and Mr. Beers went straight to the KKK men and said something to them. I don't know what.

Then Mr. Evans and Mr. Ellsworth took the cross that Father Costa had been carrying and went straight to the one burning in the sand. They used that cross to knock down the fiery one. I only saw some of that; I was watching the guns.

When one of the men started to raise his gun again, I ran out into the middle of everything, yelling for Ma and Gran'ma to get out of the way. I ran right up to the man, and for my trouble got hit across the side of the head with the gun barrel.

Just what happened after that I don't know. I suppose I was numb in the head. Later folks told me how brave I was, but I don't remember being brave. Damn foolish I was.

I must have missed a bit, because what I do remember is Dr. Hall holding my head in his lap and Mr. Peterson standing on the driver's seat of his wagon and saying something about all being one folks, just like more than two hundred years ago when his people came to Smalltown. Made a little speech, he did.

The Pranks An' Enlightenment of Frank An' Me

And Mr. Evans said something about Smalltown needing a boy to teach it bravery, willing to risk his life to save people who were white and black, Protestant and Catholic. But never for a second was I thinking I was brave; my only thoughts were for Ma and Gran'ma. I even forgot that I wasn't supposed to be there, I was so afraid that something might happen to them.

The KKK men backed off. They left town, I guess, because there never was agitation for their sort of things again. That was the end of it, and people seemed proud that they had not let such division wreck Smalltown.

I can't say that all the problems with prejudice and mistrust were solved. They weren't, not by a long shot. To me they were unspoken, but a couple of values did seem to emerge. People made it known that whatever issues might threaten Smalltown, we would deal with them ourselves without outside interference. And, whatever the feelings about different religions, there was a belated recognition of others' courage and willingness to stand for what they thought was right. Deep down even those who harbored prejudices seemed to know that the fear causing hatred was not justified. We didn't become a town full of unending tolerance; we did seem to be a town where people were trying to overcome their intolerance.

I think I started to grow up that night. I don't know if I thought of it then, but I seemed to have a considerable understanding of why men at sea sometimes risk their lives for their shipmates. I couldn't have put it into words, that's for sure, but I think I felt what it meant to want to save another person without thinking of the consequences.

You see, Smalltown was never lost, and we never lost hope, either. Just because we were not fancy did not mean that we were without purpose or lacking vitality. Our purpose was to survive as best we could and to assist our neighbors in surviving. There was no place where the Golden Rule was better acted out than Smalltown. I'll tell you about an example in a moment. It seemed

Robert Wolley

to me that just when things were looking up, along came trouble, and for Smalltown when I was a lad, trouble wasn't rum or illegals or the Klan; trouble was the Great Depression and then World War II.

It was the Great Depression that nearly did us in. I expect that is true for thousands of little towns and villages. Mostly the little people are not to blame, but mostly, too, the little people have no power. We aren't lost, but we can be losers anyway.

At that time I think that we needed the evil KKK to remind us of what we were. When Father Costa blessed the fishing boats each year, he wasn't giving a Catholic blessing to just the Catholic boats, he was giving God's blessing to all of God's fishermen, and not just fishermen but every family in Smalltown, just as when Mr. Evans and the Congregationalists ran the little store for clothes and food and gave money away that people donated, it wasn't just for their people or just for Protestants, it was for anybody in need.

I don't know this for a personal fact since it was before my time, but way back the Congregational church was called by some "The Church of the Old Order." Of course, we all know that in the beginning there was only the one church of the Pilgrim fathers and that the church was run by men only and that the men ran the town and everything. I'm not referring to the differences of doctrine, though, or to how the town was run or how you had to be a member of the church to vote in town affairs and elections or to hold office.

I'm talking about the distinction inside the church between the old, deep-water captains and their families and the coasters and fishermen and farmers and their families. The captains looked down their noses at the others.

When the Methodists came to Smalltown, there was a warm welcome. It had nothing to do with believing and everything to do with where you were on the social ladder. Not really

The Pranks An' Enlightenment of Frank An' Me

welcome in the Old Order church, the ordinary people found a religious home.

As Gran'ma used to tell it, a lot of religious groups came to Smalltown at one time or another, trying to establish a church: Baptist, Advent, Church of England, Universalist, but only the Methodist hung on.

Before my time a tiny group of Adventists came to Smalltown because Cape Cod and Smalltown were the nearest land to the rising sun. They came because they believed that the end of the world was coming on some particular date, and they wanted to be the first to greet it.

On the supposed day, whenever it was, the few of them climbed into the tallest trees which caught the sunlight first to see God destroy His creation.

Only it didn't work out that way. Gran'ma said lots of people watched those folks as they sat in the trees, making fun of them. When night came the Adventists crawled down out of the trees and left town in a hurry, kind of sheepish-like and without explaining the miscalculation, which there must have been since the world has yet to be destroyed.

And there used to be what folks called the "Come-outers." Lots of definitions have been given for that word, but what they were was a "holiness" group that had no educated or specially trained ministers, saying that the Lord would call out one of them to be the minister. That group was up in Northam, mostly. What I remember of them was that everybody claimed to be the minister, kind of like everybody on a ship claiming to be the captain.

I remember another religious group that came to Smalltown for a spell because they stayed for better than two years, as a matter of fact. The people weren't seen in town much, but they took to farming the swampland way up beyond the Harris farm, near the Pilot line. They never shopped in town, and their

Robert Wolley

children never came to school, although I don't know how they got out of that.

Like the Adventists, they came to Smalltown to wait for the end of the world. I guess they did their waiting and their calculating at the same time. Apparently they were early for the event and just farmed and made do until God ended everything. During that time, Gran'ma got to singing an old song:

> *Sailors, they got all the money,*
> *Farmers, they got naught for hay;*
> *I do love the rovin' sailor,*
> *Farmers, they may go their way.*

That verse was an old one, but Gran'ma added more:

> *Farmers, they wait till end of time,*
> *Which they say is close at hand;*
> *Sailors' girls has naught for love*
> *Till the ships come home to land.*

> *The end of life comes in a blow,*
> *As many a widow found;*
> *The end of this world is nothin'*
> *Compared to a loved one drowned.*

I can still sing that song today. At first I thought it was a kind of love song, but later I came to see that it was Gran'ma's way of making a comparison; a loved one lost is for a time the end of the world. Those religious farmers might forecast the end of the world; sailors' wives and sweethearts have experienced it many times, too many times.

The time came when the farmer group stopped farming. They had some cows and stopped milking them. You could hear

The Pranks An' Enlightenment of Frank An' Me

the poor beasts' suffering moos all over. The farmers up and gave away everything they owned, and one night they all climbed the highest dunes out near the golf course to wait for the end.

And, with the Adventists before, it didn't happen. But this time they didn't leave town. The fact is, they didn't go anywhere, didn't even leave the dunes. Two, three days they stayed there. Perhaps they figured that their calculations were a day or two off.

They never asked for help, but by the end of the third day folks got to worrying about them, especially for the children who had had no food or water for three days.

The next morning Mr. Ellsworth went to see them. They had no clothes, having given everything away except the rough sheets which went around each one. I guess there were about six or seven families; maybe two or three children each. That comes out to thirty souls.

The way I got it, Mr. Ellsworth asked the people to come into town where they'd get food and clothing and could get back some of the things they had given away. No, they said, what's given is given, and never would they ask for help or expect it.

At least send the children, begged Mr. Ellsworth. No, they said, the end of the world is at hand, although they might not see it. They would wait for the end, whenever it was.

So it went, apparently for hours. In the end it was Dr. Hall who saved them. He got his wagon filled with food and medicine and took it all up to the end-of-the-worlders. He said he was Luke, the physician, who had come to heal the believers. Finally, those folks came out of the sand and let people provide for them.

They never were the same, of course, and eventually, family by family, they drifted out of town. No one laughed at them or called them names, nothing like that. They were accepted as oddities maybe, but in spite of what people say about Cape Codders, they could have stayed and would have been welcome.

Robert Wolley

I learned a lot about toleration for religion from that time; so did everyone, but that tolerance was tested by another religious group that came to town when I was about ten.

I had never heard the word "naturist" until people began showing up in the summer. There were invitations to join the group posted on the telephone poles, something about sun worship and belief in the natural and meetings on the beach on the back shore.

I really didn't pay any attention until Frank told me that we were going to church. Another of your holidays, I asked?

"It's two words, holy days, and no, it has nothing to do with my church."

What then? And Frank filled me in, in his sometime round about way. "The state police are coming tomorrow to close the church down."

After all we had been through, that seemed ridiculous. Why, I asked, when we have churches all over? So what if someone wants to worship the sun? People have been doing that for eons.

"Oh, you poor child. Your education has been neglected. This is no ordinary worship. People do it with no clothes on." Now Frank had my attention.

"But anyone can go to their services," I protested.

"That's just it; they hold their services right on the beach where everybody else is, and a lot of people have been complaining that nude, get it, nude worshipping on a crowded beach is wrong, or should be."

"So what are the police going to do, give everyone a coat and hat?"

"Don't know. But we ought to be there to find out?"

Frank didn't have to convince me. But it wasn't the nude part, it was the prospect of seeing the state troopers that got our attention.

The Pranks An' Enlightenment of Frank An' Me

Next morning we were out on the beach early. So were a lot of others. When I was ten one went bathing, not swimming, and bathing suits, not swimming suits, were in a period of transition from the completely covered up look to something more daring. A lot of women still wore full length garments; men still wore tops and often their lower suit went to the knees; little boys might wear just short pants but by age ten tops were conventional; young girls wore fancy suits, almost sunsuits. All women except the youngest wore bonnets.

Walking on the beach we sometimes came upon an individual without any clothing, but that was rare, and always it was somewhere along the beach where other people were not expected.

But, mixed sun bathing in the nude among people on a widely used public beach was something else. It was, I think, unheard of. Thus the confrontation was a promise of something very unusual.

The morning lived up to the promise in every way possible. The naturists showed up. They sang and danced, to Frank and me looking like a bunch of old fools. The troopers showed up, looking even more foolish.

The troopers started chasing the nudes, each trooper carrying what appeared to be a blanket. When one nude was caught, he or she was wrapped in a blanket, but as soon as the trooper went after someone else, off came the first blanket. It was a Keystone comedy but better than anything we had seen in a movie.

And the regular beach goers had a ball. There wasn't a one of them that wasn't rolling in the sand laughing. And laugh we did, not at the nude people, not at the police, but simply at the absurdity of the entire scene.

One nude woman stood at the water's edge, shouting at the state police. A trooper went to arrest her. She backed into the water; he followed. When he was about to grab her, she dove under water. He tried to follow, with dire results. Heavy boots, uniform and lots of equipment discouraged swimming, and be had to be rescued by other policemen. That was the frosting on the cake.

When the police finally got some wisdom, they started gathering up all the loose, unclaimed clothing scattered over the beach. They wrapped it all in their blankets and retreated to the parking lot. Law-abiding bathers were ordered to go to their automobiles. Any automobile not claimed was ticketed. With that, the police withdrew. It was all over.

But it wasn't over. Unfortunately, Frank and I left. We were more interested in following the troopers, although their cruisers were out of sight before we even got to the road.

It was a good three miles back to town. We had seen what we went to see, so we took our time heading home, cutting across cranberry bogs, circling ponds, walking paths in the woods.

If we had stuck to the road, we would have seen the dramatic conclusion. Away from the beach, the police blocked off the road and waited. Every automobile was stopped. Anyone without proper clothing was arrested; occupants of the ticketed vehicles were arrested. And all were taken to the Legion hall, that being the only place where such a crowd could be accommodated. Frank and I missed all that.

Crane towed all the stopped automobiles to his yard; the arrested were carted off to Barnstable. We missed all that, too.

Jacob Mears and Carl Stinger had had their automobiles ticketed, the vehicles identified immediately by Crane's men. Mr. Mears and Mr. Stinger went to claim them. They had been fishing, each independently of the other, and hadn't even been aware of what had taken place. Since they had not identified their automobiles in the parking lot or made themselves known, they were assumed to have been among the unclothed.

That started a legal fuss that went on for years. Mr. Stinger and Mr. Mears had to hire a lawyer, go to a hearing, secure witnesses and generally sue the Commonwealth of

The Pranks An' Enlightenment of Frank An' Me

Massachusetts. They won, of course, and their victory started a whole slew of lawsuits which dragged out for a couple of years. Most of the words I am using now were not in my vocabulary at the time. I knew nothing of suits and the act of suing, of the crime of indecent exposure, misdemeanor, and the rest.

Fully two years after the incident on the beach, the larger issue of religious freedom was being debated by the court. Some of the naturists were claiming that their antics were religious rites protected by the Constitution. I have no idea how all of that was argued out in court, only that one day the beach was closed so that a jury could visit the scene.

Frank and I were on hand for that in our usual watching place on the dunes. We were hoping that the whole affair would be repeated for our amusement, but it wasn't. We were disappointed.

The town's folks took sides. Most were against nude bathing; some were for nude beaches set apart from the rest; some were for freedom of expression wherever one wanted to express something; others were for freedom only if it didn't bother others; some thought religion was more or less what the conventional churches preached; others thought freedom of religion included any expression whatsoever, damn the conventions.

To Frank and me it seemed silly; we weren't into the hair splitting of the arguments. I guess neither was the jury. The verdict was against nudity on public beaches on the grounds that it could wrongly influence or corrupt minors, not on the basis of freedom of worship.

The town passed an ordinance against public exposure of one's body parts, that's how the law read, and later people wanted others arrested because they exposed an arm or a knee. The entire thing, over almost three years, was one of Smalltown's least shining moments, but it did produce a lot of fun and amusement. Everyone got into the spirit of the fun, and

Robert Wolley

by making sport of the whole episode, it died a simple and natural death.

When Frank and I were born, Frank's pa and ma, being Catholic, had to go to Barnstable to attend Catholic services. Different priests came to Smalltown now and then and held services in people's homes, and then Father Costa started coming regularly. Ultimately, a little church was built.

The priest lived in a house next door to the church and had a housekeeper named Emma Sousa, an ancient, good-sized Portuguese woman. She was Father Costa's aunt. She spoke very little English, barely enough to get her grocery buying done each day.

Early one Friday morning, Frank and I were fishing off the big town pier. We hadn't caught anything but crabs, and we were feeling sorry because Frank had to have fish for his supper, being a good Catholic. Of course, his ma could have gone to Mr. Beers' place, but somehow it was worked out that Frank had to catch supper. Maybe there wasn't enough money to buy fish or maybe Frank had promised to get fish; I don't know. What I remember is that we were desperate to catch a good fish. It didn't matter any to me what Frank had to eat, but I was caught up in his need to have a Friday fish.

That is how I remember that it was a Friday, because I was asking Frank what would happen if there were no fish. I had it figured out that the Catholics had to eat fish or else, and I was asking him about the "or else" part.

Frank was explaining the best he knew how, along with wondering how in a fishing town you couldn't catch a fish, and he was telling me about certain punishments, and I was wondering what they did in the middle of Iowa for fish. Frank was going on and on, mostly about his church stuff that didn't mean too much to me, but we were having a good time at it anyway.

The Pranks An' Enlightenment of Frank An' Me

In the middle of all that, Miss Sousa came along. We figured she was out for a walk, but she went to the end of the wharf, opened a big bag she had with her, took out a handline, and threw it in. She never said a word to us, but she began talking out over the water. Frank said she was praying for a big fish for the priest's supper.

Nothing happened. I don't know what she had for bait, but it and prayer weren't working. Eventually she moved to the other side of the pier where Johnny Atwood was working on the engine of his boat.

The best we could figure it later, somehow Miss Sousa tossed her line over or around Johnny's propeller shaft. All of a sudden she yelled. At first we figured she had tied onto a fish, a pretty good one we guessed by the yell, but at the same time Johnny had cast off his dock lines and had put his boat in gear. He was pulling away from the wharf, Miss Sousa was pulling on her "fish," and the next we knew, her "fish" pulled her into the water and she was following Johnny's boat out of the harbor.

Now, there was no need for Johnny to look back. With all the noises of the boat, he couldn't hear Miss Sousa yelling or our yelling. Had he heard Miss Sousa, I don't think he would have understood the language.

Why the housekeeper didn't let go of her line is still a mystery, but either she hung on for fear of losing the Father's meal or she couldn't let go. It amounted to the same thing.

Thank the Lord Johnny was going only to his mooring. When he picked that up and shut down the engine, he must have heard the lady. Frank and I had stopped our yelling and just stood there on the pier dumb-struck and bug-eyed.

Johnny finally got it into his head to look behind the boat, although it took him a while to think to look straight down. I don't know what came to his mind when he saw a woman all dressed in black and floundering around in the water.

Robert Wolley

At long last he tossed her a line, but even Johnny could see that that was no solution. How was he going to get a halfdrowned, old lady out of the water and into his boat? Frank and I were the only witnesses to the whole thing, so what I tell you, you have to believe. There was Miss Sousa hanging on to the line Johnny had thrown her, but being old and weak, once or twice her head sank below the surface. Johnny lowered a rope ladder. We couldn't hear what was being said, but it was obvious that he was telling her to climb up. Now, that was hopeless. Rope ladders are mostly useless because all they do is swing under the boat when you put your weight on them. The rope ladder was of no use whatsoever with Miss Sousa.

Ultimately, Johnny had to jump into the water and secure Miss Sousa to the line. Then he climbed back up the ladder, not an easy task even for him. Next, we heard his winch, and he swung his net boom out over the side. There was a lot of yelling and waving by Johnny, only nothing happened. In the end, Johnny had to jump back into the water, attach the net hook to Miss Sousa, climb back up the rope ladder, and start hauling.

Miss Sousa came up very slowly, and it looked as though Johnny was landing a small blackfish because Miss Sousa always was dressed in black. It was a strange sight, to say the least. Never before had I seen a blackfish waving two arms.

When Miss Sousa was landed on deck, up started the boat, and Johnny brought her to the wharf. Poor Miss Sousa. She nearly drowned, was soaking wet, could hardly breathe, and when Frank and I grabbed Johnny's docking lines, she was yelling at Johnny and swinging her rosary beads at him.

Naturally, everything she said was in Portuguese. Johnny didn't know Portuguese, but Frank was more than willing to translate. But first he had to get Miss Sousa to shut up, which she did finally.

Then Frank started. First, he said, she said that Johnny was a dumb, stupid, ignorant, son of a poor mother who must have

The Pranks An' Enlightenment of Frank An' Me

been in pain ever since she birthed him. Frank said that was the kindest thing she said and would Johnny forgive him for not translating the other things. Then she said she was going to pray to all the saints there were in heaven to curse Johnny. Then she said that Johnny did what he did to steal her fish. There was a lot more, but Frank got to laughing.

Funny, as in strange, Emma Sousa looked just like Mary Greentree when someone made fun of her visions. If looks could have killed, Johnny and Frank and I would have been dead on the spot. Later, we came to realize how serious it all was and how lucky it was that Miss Sousa didn't drown or at least have a heart attack, but just then we had, or at least I had, only visions of a giant blackfish taking after Johnny Atwood because he stole the supper right off a priest's table. Right off we got to calling old Emma Sousa "the killerfish."

But that wasn't all. The whole affair must have caught up to her because she came near to swooning. Johnny caught her. "Get somethin'," he yelled. There wasn't anything for her to sit on that I could see, but Frank got someone's fish cart, a kind of big, two-wheel box used to move around the fish and gear. It was filled with netting and lines, but that didn't matter to Johnny. He scooped up Miss Sousa and sat her on top of everything. Miss Sousa was only half conscious.

No one else was around. Johnny figured that Miss Sousa needed Dr. Hall's attention. The wharfinger's telephone was locked in his office, so the only thing to do was to wheel the killerfish to town.

Frank and I went from moment to moment, one minute splitting our sides, the next minute worried that Miss Sousa might die and that Johnny would be blamed, he being innocent of everything.

So there's Johnny pushing the cart as fast as he can, nets and lines hanging over the edge, the killerfish on top like the prize catch of the year, and Frank and I running alongside.

Robert Wolley

We didn't meet a soul the whole way. When we got as far as Mr. Beers' place, he was out in his icehouse filleting for the market. He was pretty messy, with his rubber apron all covered with fish blood.

We paid no mind to that; the sight was a natural one, but not Miss Sousa, I guess. Mr. Beers hovered over her, we were telling him what was going on, he was telling Johnny to use the telephone to call Dr. Hall — and Miss Sousa decided to come awake fully.

What she must have seen first were all the fish blood and guts, then she must have smelled the mess, and with Mr. Beers and the rest of us hovering over her, perhaps the day seemed kind of dark. That part is speculation.

But Miss Sousa came to convinced that she was in the belly of a whale! And convinced that all of us were in that whale's belly together.

Mr. Beers knew Portuguese well enough to carry on his business and even to joke around with the fisherman who spoke Portuguese. But all the Portuguese people, except for a few old gran'parents, spoke English, so what Portuguese language Mr. Beers needed wasn't up to this. That left Frank to try to tell Miss Sousa that she wasn't in the belly of a whale, that she was at Mr. Beers' place, and that she had got wet.

I don't think she heard Frank at all because she was using her rosary beads plenty fast and praying about as loud as I ever heard, drowning out whatever Frank was saying.

Probably it wasn't Frank at all that did it, just time, because after a while Miss Sousa could tell where she was, but she never did seem to have any idea how she got there or why she was soaking wet.

All of a sudden she flopped out of the cart, and our last image of Miss Sousa was her walking up the road toward town, still soaking wet. "There, glory be, go a walkin' killerfish," said Frank.

The Pranks An' Enlightenment of Frank An' Me

"Lord Almighty, boys," moaned Johnny, "don't go ta makin' it worse than she is. Lord Almighty, that were a close one."

We got to go over the whole beginning again when the three of us tried to explain it all to Mr. Beers. Only Frank and I knew it from the beginning; not even Johnny knew how it all began, only the near sad ending.

And just as natural as breathing, the story got passed around town. Mr. Beers called Dr. Hall and relayed the story while asking him to check on Miss Sousa, so that meant that Aunt Hattie knew, and what she knew was like throwing a rooster into a pile of hens. It got everybody excited and running around. And just as natural as breathing, the story got all over town and Frank and I got to tell it many times.

Too many, it turned out, because Frank got a lecture from Father Costa about making sport of an old woman when she was in desperate trouble. Of all the people, Frank said, the Father seemed to know the least about the whole happening. And a few days after that I saw Father Costa, and he said I shouldn't be mean. I guess Frank never got to tell the priest the whole story, but since the priest had no authority over me, I said, "Hey, Father, if ya had been there, ya would have laughed too," and I went right ahead and told him what Frank and I had seen, every bit of it.

Father Costa's English lacked something, that's for sure, but I think he got a picture of the revelation. "Blackfish? Killerfish? Not nice for an old lady."

I supposed that he was right. Then he said, "Knowin' she's all right, maybe funny it is." He patted me on the head. "Maybe." I think he was beginning to visualize the whole event. He walked away muttering, "Blackfish. My, my. Killerfish? Maybe."

Robert Wolley

Chapter IX

Rumrunnin' Alice

The Pranks An' Enlightenment of Frank An' Me

There was a brief time when, for a few folks, the most prosperous business was what many called bootlegging and we called rumrunning.

I don't know how much bootleg stuff was made around here. A lot of folks made beer and wine, had been making it since the beginning of time, I suppose. That didn't amount to much, at least not enough to call particular attention to it, even when booze-making was supposed to be against the law.

But rumrunning. That's what we had here, rumrunning. Oh, some fisherman would pick up a few cases of drink here and there, and others could sometimes find a little something in the back of their automobiles or trucks. That was nothing much.

What was something were the big, powerful boats that appeared at night. Many were larger than any fishing boat in this harbor, and they were faster than lightning, with two, some said three, of the biggest engines ever made. They were what rumrunning was for a time. They came in the dead of night, charging right up to the shore all along the inner coast, and maybe a dozen men would come out of nowhere to unload them into trucks, and the trucks would shoot off into the dark to I don't know where.

And I'm not talking an occasional boat but fleets of boats that sat offshore, beyond the three-mile limit, anchored or drifting for the day, waiting for darkness. And when night came, you could hear them; they were too powerful to keep quiet.

I never went on one of the boats or talked to the men who ran them. It was nothing I ever dared to do. I stayed clear of them like sin. The boats would come into the harbors all around here, and as long as they were not carrying liquor, there was nothing anyone could do. Smalltown had a regular navy of such boats, so many that there were days when there was not enough gasoline for the local fishing boats, it all having been sold to strangers. So popular was P'town that gasoline companies brought in their lighters filled with fuel just to accommodate the traffic. It was nothing to see half a dozen lighters with boats buzzing around, all fighting to get their tanks filled. P'town was the last convenient stop before a craft headed back to Canada.

I suppose that such boats were refueled at sea on the way down the coast because loaded as they were with spirits, I can't believe that they could have carried enough gasoline.

I never knew any of the men who ran rum boats. I did know many of the men who unloaded them. My own pa, and Cloyd, and others, too, some of Smalltown's church supporters and best citizens, were regular unloaders. Everybody knew who was doing that. It was no secret.

In fact, it was more like playing a game. The fact that every man, woman and child knew about it might have meant, since nobody did anything really to stop it, that all the foolishness in the dark could have been done in broad daylight — if it weren't for the government men. They were what made it interesting. The landings and times and routes had to be kept a secret from them. That was the game part.

Why, I would see men all ganged up, ready to jump a rumrunning bunch, and then when they had done that, the posse, or whatever you want to call it, would spend the whole night drinking up the evidence. My pa was partial to getting rid of the evidence. Now, that's what I call playing games.

And one more thing to bring it around. I said that I never knew any of the men who ran the rum boats, but I knew one woman from Smalltown who did some pretty fancy running.

Her name was Alice something-or-other. What I mean is, I don't remember what name she had before she came to Smalltown. That was way before I was born, somewhere around 1910 or 1915. She came from New York and set up a studio of sorts on the Depot Road where she designed fabrics and ladies' clothing.

The Pranks An' Enlightenment of Frank An' Me

She must have done a lot of business because she traveled between Smalltown and New York often; even when I was small I remember seeing her board the afternoon train to Boston. She was always dressed poorly, although people said that she had lots of money. Folks liked her; she was a character of sorts, and when she first came to Smalltown she took all our peculiar ways, at least what outsiders thought were peculiar, and our ways of talking and such and exaggerated them to the point where no one knew what she was except some kind of humorous joke on ourselves.

Now that's what I had always heard, and I rightly think it was so. At first folks didn't think kindly of Alice-whatever, but by the time I remember her she was pretty much like the rest of us and was getting along fine around town, serving on town committees and the like. I first recall her when she was middle-aged. She was still working and I can remember ladies praising her designs and her clothing and asking about her trips to New York.

Sometime before liquor was made illegal, she must have lost her job because she started working around town and didn't go to New York any more. She had an automobile, made by the Dodge Brothers, that she sold, and she sold all of her land except her house lot. She seemed right poor, just like the rest of us.

At the time of my earliest recollections, she wasn't married, but she was very friendly with Paul Abbey, the butcher from the First National.

A widower, Mr. Abbey was a great big man who could lift a whole body of beef, five or six hundred pounds. He came to Smalltown from Ireland, people used to say, where he was supposed to have killed a man in a fight. I never knew if that was true and didn't think so because he said he was born in Boston and married a Boston lady. She was another who died giving birth, and the baby died, too. A man wouldn't make up a story like that.

Robert Wolley

Some said he just messed around for a time after that and ended up in Smalltown; others said he traveled around the world some as a seaman, fought in every bar around the world, then ended up in Ireland and killed a man, and then sneaked home and ended up in Smalltown. I don't know anything about that.

Summertime, men always were looking for live minnows for bait, and Frank and I ran a pretty good business off the railroad bridge over the creek. We had a large square net made out of cheesecloth and wire and always managed a few bones and meat scraps from Mr. Abbey for minnow bait. We liked him for that.

Whatever the truth of his early years, Mr. Abbey was a grand man. He was somewhere between Ma and Gran'ma's age, but what made him grand, besides his gentle manner and good looks, was his touring automobile and his giving pleasure to anyone who wanted to ride with him. He had been in Smalltown a long while and knew every crook and cranny of it. There wasn't a square inch of Smalltown and hereabouts that he didn't know, and he had made a two-wheel path to almost every one of those spots. Most of the roads in and around Smalltown today were first laid out by Mr. Abbey. He'd just drive right into the sand or the woods with his vehicle to see how far he could go and where, and if he got stuck, well, that was half the fun.

Frank and I loved to go exploring with Mr. Abbey, and so did a lot of people, young and old. Mr. Abbey's automobile never was empty for long. Want the best wild cranberries or the best beach plums or the most bayberries or the pond with the biggest pickerel or the beach with the most seaclams? Mr. Abbey knew them all. He knew where the old shipwrecks were along the shore and where the prettiest pond lilies were, and lady slippers and jack-in-the-pulpits. He could show you monster turtles. A trip with Mr. Abbey was exciting learning, all within a range of seven or eight miles.

Paul Abbey and Alice whatever-her-name-was were right friendly. Anybody and everybody got to ride with Mr. Abbey in

The Pranks An' Enlightenment of Frank An' Me

the daytime, but only Alice got to ride with him at night. Folks seemed to figure they would or, when I look back on it, they should get married. There was always a lot of gossip about their carrying on.

But that marrying never happened. All of a sudden, somehow Alice got herself married to a man over in Barnstable named Hargood, so she became Alice Hargood, and that's how I knew her most of her life.

Mr. Hargood was what my Gran'ma used to call "a grand merchant." In Barnstable he had stores that sold dry goods and lumber, and he owned some kind of fishing business. Again, all this I learned later. I never saw the man. I guess nobody around here did either because he died only weeks after marrying Alice what's-her-name. For the life of me, I can't remember what her name was before it was Hargood.

Maybe it was a good thing that Mr. Hargood died because Mr. Abbey was fit to be tied. When Alice told him she was marrying someone else, Mr. Abbey carried on something awful, even threatening to kill her and Mr. Hargood. I didn't see it, but I guess he busted up his own place behind the post office, then busted up Alice's house. Finally he even busted up part of the First National. I saw that damage. And then he lit out of town.

Don't that beat all? What it did, of course, was give some credence to all the stories about Mr. Abbey and Ireland.

Now, Alice was gone only a few weeks before coming home a widow. She acted like a rich old hag, only it turned out that she wasn't rich at all. It seems that Mr. Hargood had been married a couple of times before and had a slew of children and had gone and made up a new will before marrying Alice and had left everything except the fishing business to his children.

What he left Alice were two fishing boats, leaving the fish pier and the fish house and all that went with them to his children.

Robert Wolley

So Alice got nothing but two fishing boats, and there was hardly a living being made fishing. She went from thinking she was rich to being poor again in just a couple of weeks, and not only poor but with the upkeep of two fishing boats that weren't earning a penny.

Alice Hargood couldn't sell the boats, and nobody wanted to fish for her, so she was stuck with two pretty good boats but with nothing to do with them but to let them swing at their moorings. She even had to pay for new moorings.

Why she brought them to Smalltown and tried to sell them here was beyond comprehension. There was no market here. She should have tried in Barnstable, but I suppose she didn't know better. Thus, the boats sat in the water for a long time, and Smalltown was no place to keep a boat in the water over the winter, what with ice three or four feet thick in the harbor moving up and down, in and out every minute of the day and night. Ice like that can saw a boat nearly in two, or if the ice gets thick enough, it can lock a boat in slowly and crush it.

Alice was lucky the first winter; there wasn't too much ice, and the damage to her boats was not too great, although she did have considerable damage to the engines and pipes which she had neglected to winterize.

Alice had two boats, one maybe thirty-five or thirty-six feet, made up in Nova Scotia, the other larger, maybe forty-five feet, made in Boston, and in the spring, March or April, around Easter time, a man from P'town came to look at the big boat and bought it. He cheated Alice something awful. Mr. Beers and others said that the boat and all the fishing gear was worth at least three thousand dollars. The man paid only five hundred.

But maybe Alice knew that because part of the bargain was for the man to fix up the Novie boat and, and this is the best part, teach Alice to run it. So maybe Alice got herself a bargain. The Novie got to running just fine, and Alice did learn to run it pretty well. Except when it came to docking it. The fishermen got to calling her "Feel-for-it-Alice" because of the way she came into the wharf. She would approach real slow, as if she was hoping that the dock would come to her. Then, when she was almost there, she always gave too much power and always smacked hard.

Alice didn't use her boat for fishing but put up signs offering to take people for sightseeing tours on a real fishing boat. She did that but one year. The Coast Guard found out that she had no license and her boat had no life-saving equipment and a bunch of other violations. She was fined and put out of her sightseeing business.

By coincidence, when the Coast Guard shut down Alice's tour business was when rumrunning was reaching its height. Alice just shifted gears. That wouldn't make much of a story other than a woman piloting one of the scores of rumrunners of Cape Cod. Probably there were other women doing just that, but not like our Alice.

When rumrunning first started around here there weren't too many in it, not from Smalltown anyway, and it was dangerous with all the Federal's aiming to keep people pure and honest.

After Alice's sightseeing business got shut down, she went away for a spell, and when she came back she had two men with her. They stayed in her house, going out in the boat almost every day and lots of nights. I supposed they were learning the boat's workings from Alice. That was near Labor Day as I recall.

What I remember about the two men is that they always wore fancy men's hats and always wore a shirt and tie and dark suits, even when it was warm. That was strange and made them strange. They never spoke to anyone, Alice always doing the talking if there was need.

Anyway, winter came and the boat was gone and the men with it, and Frank and I figured that was the last we'd ever see of either, supposing that Alice had sold the Novie to the two men. How wrong we were.

It was March again before we saw Alice's boat, only this time we heard it before we saw it. We found out that it had been repowered with two engines, overpowered really, because the few times we caught it going full blast it was the fastest thing we had ever seen. Folks speculated about the speed but couldn't agree, although forty-five mph was accepted generally. I don't know myself how fast it was.

What I know is that the boat jumped out of the water with just the very stern and the props in the water, and when it did that, the whole boat twisted one way or the other in the air, always coming down with a crash. One wave or one wrong twist and it was goodbye. The other thing that got our attention was that no boat could take that abuse for long. Sooner or later it was going to shake or bang itself apart.

The reconstruction of that boat entailed taking all of the fishing gear away and leaving a clear deck broken only by a couple of hatch covers. We assumed that the fish holds had been cleaned and converted to..., well, we didn't know what.

Up to then there had been no evidence to suppose that Alice was into anything having to do with transporting liquor. And yet there was evidence to convict her, at least for Frank and me to presume her guilt. The greatest bit of evidence were the same two men who had been with Alice the previous fall. They returned with her. They never seemed to leave the boat and must have slept on it and eaten on it. Even handling the boat they wore the same suits and hats we had seen before.

But, and this was our evidence, under their suits they were wearing guns. More than once when the men were at close range, Frank and I saw the guns tucked up under their armpits.

One thing was sure, when the Novie was loaded down with booze it didn't jump out of the water; it just flattened out and

The Pranks An' Enlightenment of Frank An' Me

went hell-bent-for-election. No government boat was ever close in speed. But I've gotten ahead of myself.

Alice did enter the rumrunning business and landed her boat all up and down the coast on our part of the Cape and in places where no one would have guessed it was possible to land or where trucks big enough to carry the cargo could get. Alice never landed in the same place twice, but always there were the tracks of the trucks, and for those who were trying to catch the rumrunners, other evidence of landings.

The area around Smalltown became saturated with liquor. For a time the government men questioned everybody in town. Only someone who knew the Cape like the back of his hand could plan all the landings. In our neck of the woods the only person who fit that image was Paul Abbey, but Mr. Abbey had been gone for some time, ever since Alice decided to marry Mr. Hargood, and he hadn't been seen or heard from since. It seemed that Mr. Abbey was a good suspect but an unlikely one. Then one night, on the back road out of Smalltown to Northam, there was a gun fight. A man was shot, and that man was Paul Abbey.

By the time I learned about it, Mr. Abbey was at Dr. Hall's being fixed up. There was speculation everywhere about everything and questions galore. Should Dr. Hall turn Mr. Abbey over to the police? Was Mr. Abbey working with Alice Hargood? Was he leading a rival gang trying to take over from Alice and her cohorts? Was he the one who had arranged all the landings? For Alice? For others, but not for Alice?

No one knew the Cape like Mr. Abbey, so working for or with Alice seemed a likely explanation. So, too, did the theory that he was leading an Irish gang and that the other gang was Italians. There were few Italians around our part of the Cape, and what we knew about them was all second-hand and mostly bad, gangster-like because of all the newspaper stuff.

Naturally, because no one knew anything positive, it made it easy to imagine everything and to blame those about whom we knew the least. So, for a couple of days, we talked about Irish gangs and Italian gangs, and that kind of sidetracked us from Alice Hargood.

Somebody told about Mr. Abbey. He wasn't hurt badly, more pain than anything, I guess, and the state police took him away. But, we learned later, he spent only a few days in jail.

It wasn't long after that that one night, I know this because Frank and I saw the ending of it, Alice fetched her load up Blackfish Creek, the tidal creek that separates Smalltown and Northam and was so named because forever the blackfish have been beaching themselves there at the head.

The upper head of the creek can be navigated only at certain high tides throughout the year. Blackfish beachings up the creek have been happening since before the Indians came here. The Indians made good use of the creatures, and so did the Pilgrims and everyone else until whale oil wasn't needed for lamps and cooking. The blackfish still come, only now they're called pilot whales. Sometimes they're a few; sometimes hundreds beach themselves at the same time.

That night Alice was to unload her Novie at the head of Blackfish Creek at high tide. And that night a great pod of blackfish decided to kill themselves in the same spot.

Lots of fish must have gotten themselves on the beach before Alice nosed her boat onto the muddy shore. And while Alice was working her way in, lots of fish must have come in behind her. Why Alice didn't see the fish is beyond me, but even if she couldn't see them, she must have heard them breathing. Being whales, they blow every few minutes, and with the great number there must have been an awful lot of blowing noise. Of course, her boat made some racket, so maybe she couldn't hear after all.

With all the fish, they being twelve, fifteen feet long and weighing half a ton or more, strewn all over the edge of the small beach, removing Alice's cargo must have been impossible.

The Pranks An' Enlightenment of Frank An' Me

Apparently the landing was planned at the height of the tide and counted on the boat being much lighter to get out of the creek even an hour after high tide, but so many blackfish piled in behind the Novie, backing the boat off became impossible. That's my theory, anyway. Alice and her friends must have panicked.

Come sun up, it was all there. Boxes of liquor were all over the place, lots of them smashed from being dropped among scores of dead and dying blackfish. Alice's boat was high and dry in the mud surrounded by the little whales.

There's a road not far from the head of the creek, and sure enough, someone came along and saw the peculiar sight. Soon everyone in town knew about it, and just about everybody in town went to see what was going on, for lots of reasons.

Some went to do a little beachcombing, taking what the Great Provider had delivered. Some went because the blackfish would soon be a serious health hazard, not only stinking up the neighborhood but rotting with who knows what disease and attracting all kinds of unpleasant creatures. Some went to see what boat it was and maybe salvage a little something from it. Some went out of plain old-fashioned curiosity, like Frank and me, because it was an adventure.

Alice wasn't around, nor were the two creepy men with the guns that were always with her. But guess who was guarding the boat. Right. Mr. Abbey.

Mr. Abbey's explanation was that he was coming along the road and saw everything and was just doing his dear friend a good deed by protecting Alice Hargood's property. He was as amazed as anyone that liquor was there, assuming that Alice's boat must have drifted off its mooring. The boat and the liquor were a startling coincidence, hardly enough proof to even suggest that Alice had a hand in rumrunning.

The amount of liquor on the beach would have bought a small fleet of boats like Alice's. With all the blackfish, carrying out the liquor in their heavy cases was practically impossible in the dark, although from the looks of it, broken cases and all, it had been tried. No one would have been foolish enough to bring men and trucks for the liquor in broad daylight, so the stuff just sat there, although many a single case got carried away to be hidden in Smalltown and Northam houses. Actually, over the course of the day, it was surprising how the supply dwindled. Particularly prized was Canadian whiskey. Even Frank's father came to have some, and he was supposed to be dead set against drink.

The end of it for that day was the arrival of the government men. They came for the liquor, but they also arrested Mr. Abbey and, later, Alice. I don't know what happened to the two men always with Alice. The government posted a guard on Alice's boat and finally got it out of the creek. Most of the blackfish were burned in an awesome fire, and everything was plowed under the beach later into gigantic holes.

A trial was held in Barnstable soon thereafter. Frank and I didn't get to go, of course, but everybody talked about it and we got pretty good information.

Mr. Abbey was tried first, and while there was a great to-do about how he and Alice schemed the whole thing, the jury believed Mr. Abbey's story, especially since a couple of Smalltown men were on the jury and remembered the terrible things Mr. Abbey had said and done when Alice married the Barnstable man. They must have figured there was no way Mr. Abbey and Alice could have patched things up.

Next Alice got tried. First she made out that the two mysterious men, and she gave them names, were cousins from New York who had used her boat and house for vacationing. When that didn't go over too well, she allowed as how they had forced her to take part in the illegal business. She got none too much sympathy for that line either. Then she said that she and Mr. Abbey had patched things up, and because she was blinded by love, she did what he told her. She laid the whole blame on him.

But he had been tried and couldn't be tried again because of double something or other, and when he was called as a witness to Alice's claims, he just kept saying he didn't know anything.

It was while Alice was trying to put it all on Mr. Abbey that she told about making so many deliveries to all the out of the way spots that were so good. And why were they so good? Because over the years Mr. Abbey had made the paths to them or knew how to reach them without getting stuck in the sand or lost in the dark.

People got to believing that Mr. Abbey was guilty after all, and there was nothing they could do about it. What made it seem so logical was when Alice told about the gun fight. That wasn't a gun fight at all, according to Alice, but just a lot of shooting by Paul Abbey and his friends intended to scare off anybody who might have ideas about highjacking. Mr. Abbey shot himself by mistake.

The first time around, the jury couldn't agree about what Alice told. They all agreed that she had been running stuff, but they couldn't agree on just which laws she had broken since there were no witnesses that ever actually saw her doing the running. And if there were no witnesses, the jury wondered if there was a crime. It was a hung jury. Alice was set free knowing that she would go to trial again.

Since she had not been proven guilty, there was a hot debate in the courtroom about whether her boat should continue to be impounded, and if it was, who would pay to take care of it. Cape Cod thriftiness, you could call it, finally decided that Alice would get her boat back while she was waiting for a new trial. I told you before that this whole business was something of a game. I half expected Pa and Cloyd to become part of Alice's mess.

Alice got her boat back to Smalltown, and for a time nothing happened. In the late fall Frank came to the house all excited. He was working on one of the fishing boats, and when he went to the boat before sunup, Alice's boat was gone from the harbor. And when he came back at nightfall, Alice's boat was still gone.

I suggested that since it was getting along in the season the boat was probably being hauled out somewhere for the winter. Maybe, said Frank, but he didn't think so, and neither did the fishermen. They all thought that Alice had gone back to work again. Naw, I said, she wouldn't do that, not with her trial still to come up.

How wrong I was. All by herself she had made a deal with suppliers off Race Point. That was a pretty fair trip alone, and with the delivery probably being made at night, a dangerous one, to say nothing about Alice dealing with some very rough and tough people.

But Alice got her load, and a good one it was. I don't know where she was going to unload it, but she was on her way when, can you believe this, she ran into a government boat.

I mean ran into it! In the dark of night it was just sitting dead in the water with no lights showing, and Alice hit it. Of course, Alice was arrested. Now there was a boatload of evidence and a bunch of witnesses.

Poor Alice. Arrested again. Two days later she was being tried, in Barnstable again. This time her lawyer's argument was that she couldn't be tried because she was waiting an earlier trial, and that one came first.

Right away the government dropped the first charges, so that argument cut no bait. But again the jury couldn't agree. One of the jurymen argued that the government boat was guilty of crimes, not showing proper lights and not signaling and not making any attempt to get out of Alice's way, and that it was not fair for Alice to be tried if the government was guilty. The argument about maritime law prevailed, and enough of the jury agreed with the gentleman to hang the jury again.

The Pranks An' Enlightenment of Frank An' Me

In retrospect, I think the jury was less concerned with Alice's guilt or innocence than with what today might be called making an existentialist point. It put the government prosecutors in their place, and it called into question the matter of an individual's freedom compromised by another's misconduct, in this case breaking maritime laws. There was no doubt about Alice Hargood's crimes, nor was there much question about the jury being duty-bound to uphold the law, but judgment was going to be rendered correctly and properly. Even one as blatantly guilty as Alice should be judged fairly. Taking away an individual's precious freedom was too serious a matter to be taken lightly or improperly.

Out of all the police and court business, Alice emerged as a kind of Robin Hood-like heroine, only she had never given anything to the poor or robbed the rich. She was an outlaw character who was an outlaw because of what most people saw as a stupid law. The only ones benefiting from the laws of prohibition were real criminals and liquor-makers in Canada and elsewhere.

Alice was on the beach for good just waiting for certain punishment when the right jury came along. So what did she do? The only natural thing; she got herself a job driving a rum truck, and, of course, she got caught somewhere near Fall River. For that she went to Framingham prison for a year and a half.

She never did go to trial for the other things. The law was reversed, and Alice was ignored. She came back to Smalltown for a while, but it was too tame. I never saw her again. Folks said that she went off to some western state and got herself in more trouble. She did give us some excitement, though, and Frank and I talked about it for a good long while.

Robert Wolley

Chapter X

Some Navigation

The Pranks An' Enlightenment of Frank An' Me

I want to tell you about some fancy navigation on Frank's part.

One day a man came by as Frank and I were mending nets for Mr. Mann. Herman Mann was in his nineties, and Joshua Kingman, Mr. Mann's longtime crew, was in his seventies. How they managed their boat and nets always amazed us.

All that spring we had fished on weekends with the two old men, and I thought we might have a permanent summer job. With but one more year of schooling, Frank and I talked about owning Mr. Mann's boat someday, figuring that neither of the old men could possibly continue to fish. We had come to know their boat well. *Gertie* was an old-timer, stout, well-powered, and maintained better than any boat in the harbor. Neither man could remember where the name came from, but Mr. Kingman swore it was one of Mr. Mann's frequent girlfriends. They'd argue about it for hours.

The man, a Mr. Winters, came along and asked Frank and me to take him tuna fishing. We told him we didn't own the boat, which he probably had figured out for himself anyway. We also told him that tuna were a long way out if he wanted yellowfin, but he said no, he wanted school tuna, what we called horse mackerel. He was quite honest about his needs, telling us that he liked to fish, that he had never fished for anything of any size in the salt water, and that he was afraid of the ocean.

He was determined to overcome his fear, thinking that a sizable fishing boat like Gertie would be better than one of the sport fishing boats in Barnstable or Provincetown. Bigger is better, he said. I wasn't sure that such a trite thought was true, but I held my tongue on that matter and directed him to Mr. Mann's house up on Depot Avenue. Frank figured that was the last of Mr. Winters.

He was back in short order. "You boys know how to run that thing?"

"Yes, Sir."

"You could find the tuna?"
"Couldn't guarantee that."
"Mr. Mann says he won't take me fishing."
"Then that's the end of it," Frank said.
"No, just the beginning. He said I could work a deal with you two, if you were willing. He also said you were as good as they come."

I figured that last bit was just plain flattery. It was not like Mr. Mann or any other boat owner to let someone else use his boat, and two boys at that, even if those two boys were about to finish their schooling. I made Frank go up to see Mr. Mann and get straight exactly what he had said to Mr. Winters.

While Frank was gone, Mr. Winters asked a lot of questions, most of them had to do with things such as age and experience. "I run a heavy machinery company," Mr. Winters explained. "Hire a bunch of kids like you and your friend. Some are lousy, some are good, and some are exceptional, and I would trust them with almost everything except the cranes. Mr. Mann really placed you and the other lad in the exceptional category. How long have you been working the boats?"

When I told him that Frank and I had been working on the fishing boats since we were eleven, he was impressed. "But," I cautioned him, "what we did at eleven was nothin' but chores. We never did none of the actual runnin' of the boat or the fishin'."

"But you were learning."

"Yes, we watched everythin' an' learned by gradually doin' bits of everythin'."

"That's the best kind of education. But when you're out on the water, how do you know where you are or where you're going?"

I tried to explain. "When you go on the boats, it's expected that you'll learn how to run 'em. Every man or boy is expected to learn that right off. Then you're expected to be able to pilot

The Pranks An' Enlightenment of Frank An' Me

the boat home, no matter where you are. You learn the compass an' how to use the charts before you learn anythin' else. It's never spoken, but it's expected that if anythin' happens, you can take care of your shipmates an' the boat."

I don't think that I exaggerated; we did learn by doing. And by constant reinforcement of what we were taught. Fathom lines are a big deal for fishermen. The ocean bottom has its ups and downs just like the land, and since fish are seldom found in the middle depths, knowing how deep the water is and where the deep holes and shallows are is critical. Good charts are essential, but one has to know how to read them. Boat speed, running time, distance made over the bottom, direction, all must be recorded and entered into one's navigation. Bearings, reciprocals, triangulation, all essential knowledge and practical application. Since our town was so closely tied to marine affairs, much of our schooling took that into consideration, especially geography and math.

Mr. Winters was an appreciative audience. I was even beginning to impress myself when, in truth, much of what I knew I couldn't remember ever having learned as such in a specific lesson. I do recall that algebra was both easy and of immediate use. Cape children always did well with algebra, and I suppose that was because of its immediate application and practicality. We had been doing many of the problems without giving them an academic name.

Luckily, Frank returned before I pontificated further. I was beginning to sound rather stupid but didn't know how to turn my speech-making off.

"It's true," Frank reported. "Mr. Mann said he wasn't feelin' well an' that Mr. Kingman were in Barnstable 'cause Mrs. Kingman was taken ta the hospital. Mr. Mann said we was ta stop with the nets. He might not be fishin' for a time. An' he said we was trusted 'bout as much as any two men. If we wanted, we can strike a deal with Mr. Winters for not less than two hundred dollars, take the gas money out of it, an' split the rest 70/30. Mr. Mann gets the 70 part 'cause he's got ta split with Mr. Kingman."

That certainly was welcome, that any one would have that much faith in us. I let that sink in for a few minutes. Then I asked, "What's that mean?" I knew Frank had already figured it out.

"At two hundred dollars, that's one hundred forty dollars for Mr. Mann and sixty dollars for us."

"You didn't figure in the gasoline money."

"We'll charge extra for that. Fill up the tank, which'll come out of Mr. Mann's share, an' fill up 'gain when we return. The man will have to pay for that, which we'll give to Mr. Mann, an' the food."

"That'll cost 'im close to three hundred dollars maybe."

"Take it or leave it we'll tell 'im."

We kept Mr. Winters waiting while we discussed the deal. The money was important, but we kept debating the item of even greater importance, our use of Mr. Mann's boat. There was no doubt in our minds of the step we were about to take. For a couple of years we had told each other how ready we were to captain any boat; now the opportunity was before us, and we had doubts, serious doubts.

"Sure was nice of Mr. Mann," I said, skirting the issue.

"He was real flatterin', that's for sure."

"I'm hopeful that we're doin' the right thin'."

"We could tell Mr. Winters ta check with us tomorrow." I could see doubt written all over Frank's face.

"No. We got ta decide."

"Sink or swim?"

"Well," I said, "I was rather thinkin' fish or cut bait."

Frank was quiet for a few seconds, then he asked, "If ya had ya choice of all the boats in the harbor, which one would ya like to have?"

The Pranks An' Enlightenment of Frank An' Me

"The Missus," I answered. "Or Gertie."

"We ain't got the Missus. But we got Gertie, if we take her."

"And who would be the captain?" It was a practical question. Only one of us could be boss, not withstanding that we had never faced this question before. "We can't both be the captain."

"We'll toss for it." Frank fumbled in his pockets for a coin. He didn't have one, nor did I.

"Look," I said. "You be the captain."

"Naw, I'll let you have the honor."

"Then we'll throw fingers, two out of three. You call."

Frank called even and won the first toss. He called even again, and again he won. It was settled; Frank was the captain of our first expedition alone.

Mr. Winters agreed to the price without batting an eye. He had two friends he wanted to join him, so maybe it would cost each one only a hundred dollars. I said that with great respect because I had never seen a hundred dollars.

"One more thin'," I said to Mr. Winters. "You will have to bring your own food."

"And no liquor," Frank added with emphasis on the negative.

"Agreed. We'll even bring food for the two of you. As for liquor, I just know that I'm going to be seasick, so don't worry about drinking."

"A lot of seasickness be in the mind," said Frank.

"Son, I've heard that before. Believe me, I've fished on the Great Lakes and some mighty big rivers, and I've always been sick. The damnable thing is, I have a passion for sport fishing, always have, ever since I was a tiny tot, and I always get sick. I'll survive."

"Well, eat a good breakfast. No greasy stuff," Frank advised, "and no coffee."

Robert Wolley

The wind was blowing twelve or fifteen knots the next morning and promised to be higher by afternoon. The three men looked uncomfortable but decided to go out.

Gertie was a working trawler, not a sport fishing boat, and the decks were cluttered with winches and pulleys and lines and nets, everything dangerous to someone not used to them. Frank and I had picked up and organized as best we could. We even had rigged up some lines for hanging on to and for keeping the men away from some of the gear. We had tied down some crates for sitting, but hanging on to a two hundred fifty-pound tuna, if we were lucky enough, was going to be a real stunt in a seaway. Gertie's aft rails and transom were cut extremely low so that the nets could be drawn up on the afterdeck and so that water and garbage could flow overboard. For all practical purposes, anyone falling down without holding on to something would or could be washed overboard. We rigged lines for the men, also.

Mr. Winters and his friends showed up with enough fishing gear to outfit a dozen boats. We had suggested Peterson's as the most likely source for equipment, and Mr. Peterson must have outdone himself in the sales department. I had been working in his store for years, and I didn't even know that he had such stock. Half of what the men brought aboard I had never seen before, anywhere.

There were two techniques for catching tuna that I knew. One was to troll with large, flashy spoons and with what are called "teasers," big, pretty plugs that are supposed to get the tuna's attention and get him to look at the spoons. The other was to chum the water with fish blood and guts and offer the tuna sizable chunks of fresh fish with hooks embedded in them.

Neither of us had much idea where to go. The horse mackerel were all over Massachusetts Bay, but they were never in big schools, just strung out in what Mr. Prince used to call "a loose confederation."

The Pranks An' Enlightenment of Frank An' Me

Frank said that we should make a short drag and get enough of whatever we caught for chum. I agreed, if we could figure out what to do with our three "swells."

What we did was make them all helmsmen. Actually, we had to; it was going to be all Frank and I could do to manage the net. They got a kick out of that, and we had a successful first drag, enough to make chum for a whole month. Frank cut while I finished securing the nets and lines on the drums. The wind was increasing, and we wanted nothing that wasn't tied down.

The three men were delighted with our trawl, even if it did take a long time. I could see that Alice Hargood had had a good idea once in charging people to ship on her fishing boat. Too bad she hadn't actually fished. To a first-timer, it was an exciting adventure. The only problem we had was being sure that each man had his time at the wheel, and that he kept a reasonably straight course.

When Frank announced that we had a barrel of blood and guts, we let the boat drift, baited lines out. Boy, did Gertie roll. Even I said that, and I was known to have particularly good sea legs. Mr. winters and his friends lasted about half an hour. They'd had enough of that. Rolling, fish gunk, and the smell of fish parts conspired to unsettle the stomachs of the uninitiated. I had never seen green faces, but I was beginning to imagine that I could on Mr. Winters.

We trolled for a while, Frank throwing out chum all along the way. As long as we quartered the waves, Gertie settled into a nice, easy rolling gait. About eleven o'clock, I decided to have lunch. Frank, too. The others elected to forego the nice sandwiches they had provided. I told Mr. Winters that full stomachs were happy stomachs, but he didn't believe me.

We had caught nothing and decided to run closer to shore where the shoaling began. It would be rougher but maybe more fruitful.

Suddenly, one of the men let out a yell: fish on! Then there was another yell. Two tuna at once. We tied lines around each man's waist and brought in the teasers and the third line. Far back we thought we could see fish break the surface.

For thirty minutes a battle raged, which makes it sound a little too dramatic perhaps, but as Frank held the boat into the wind, the men pumped, then lost line, and pumped again. There certainly was a lot of excitement. I felt sorry that Mr. Winters had not hooked up, but after a bit, one of the others gave Mr. Winters his place. I couldn't see that an inch of line had been gained, even though all three men were working as hard as they could.

I went up into the wheelhouse. "I ain't never seen fish act like this," I told Frank. "Don't run sideways any and don't give or take much either way."

Frank had a big grin. "Look hard, dummy. We ain't got no fish. We've hooked onto a lobster pot line for sure, probl'y a good one with plenty of pots for heft."

"What we gonna do?"

"Give 'em 'nother few minutes an' then break off."

Both lines parted at about the same time. Frank had slowly increased the boat's speed. In the waves, no one noticed, but the strain was too much for the lines. "Too bad," Frank yelled. "They must of got tangled up together."

The men were disappointed and enthused at the same time, and Frank and I went into an act of utter disappointment and empathy.

"Gawd," Mr. Winters shouted, "they was whoppers! Did you ever see anything fight like that?"

The trip was a success, topped off when Frank asked if they wanted to try for stripers on the way home.

"I want another chance at them tuna," Mr. Winters said.

The Pranks An' Enlightenment of Frank An' Me

"Have ta be 'nother day," Frank told him. "Time ta be headin' in. But we got one rip ta skirt an' might jest tie inta a big old striper."

Which was done; five in fact, while almost losing the boat doing it. Fishing a rip with a forty-two foot trawler is damn foolish. The currents can twist you before you can react, and you need plenty of power to come about and move against currents of great force. The idea is to stand off, stern first to the rip, and cast into it. We did that successfully and landed our five bass. But somehow Frank let the bow swing toward the shallows.

The current caught us broadside. We were instantly into the green water, the current sweeping us toward unending and unthinkable trouble.

Only the fact that Mr. Mann had a right good engine saved our skins. Frank gave every bit of power Gertie had, and I truly believed it was not enough. I could see the bottom, and I'm sure we plowed a stretch of it before the boat came about enough to angle out. We had to charge through the breakers, but they were the least of our worry at the moment.

We never told Mr. Mann about that, and I don't think the men knew how close to disaster we had been. Frank and I tried to act as though the whole bit was natural, just another part of the normal fisherman's day. I guess we were convincing, but it's not every day that two people are on the wheel.

But we got home safely, no thanks to Frank. Needless to say, he was contrite of heart. Later, I asked him if he had prayed. No, he said, he had been too busy and too scared. But, he added, he might have to confess, to Father Costa, and that was okay because the Father knew nothing of boats and green water.

Mr. Winters gave us two hundred sixty-three dollars, sixty-three of it for gasoline. Then each man gave us ten extra, so Frank and I made ninety for the day, forty-five each, which was not too bad, I'd say. And Mr. Mann was thankful for his share, telling us how delighted he was that we had had a successful and uneventful trip.

Even when we were giving Mr. Mann his money and telling him about the "tuna" and the bass, neglecting to say just how we had caught the bass, we were a bit unsteady, but that disappeared somewhat when he told us how proud he was of us because he knew that we would take good care of Gertie.

For a long time we wondered if in fact we had betrayed his trust in us. Frank and I decided that some things were not worth telling. We had learned a valuable lesson, one that would be remembered always. We had been tested by our own stupidity. That Frank had been at the helm did not lessen my share of the blame; I had eagerly agreed to fish the rip; I was not as alert as I should have been. Later, there were times when I wish I had been at the wheel, not that I would have done differently but to relieve Frank of some of the burden of guilt. He took that experience hard. In time he was able to work out of his depression and see the whole thing for what it was, two boys learning to be responsible men.

Mr. Mann was particularly delighted by our rendition of the tuna hooking, and as we acted it out for him, we could see a sparkle in his eyes. "Damn good, boys. Damn good."

We had promised to have the stripers gutted and iced for Mr. Winters, and early the next morning he and his friends came to Gertie for their catch. They were still talking about the fish that got away.

I told Mr. Winters to talk with Mr. Mann if they wanted to go again, but it never came about. Mrs. Kingman died the very next day. Mr. Kingman moved away shortly after that, and Mr. Mann never did go fishing again and sold his boat, one I had come to respect, to a party in Sayersville.

When we were saying goodbye to Mr. Winters, I asked him if he had received his money's worth. More than enough, he said.

The Pranks An' Enlightenment of Frank An' Me

"And I was scared the whole time. I kept watching you two lads, so full of confidence, so sure of yourselves, and I forgot sometimes how petrified I was. I even forgot to be sick, and I always get seasick."

"I'd give back ya money just to hear them nice things," Frank offered.

"Really?" Mr. Winters asked.

"Well...." Frank never did complete the thought, but I knew what he meant.

Robert Wolley

Chapter XI

Jess Potter: "It's a No Go, Moe"

The Pranks An' Enlightenment of Frank An' Me

    I have already told you about Jess Potter attempting to save Grace Willis's prized goods when her house was burning to the ground. Now, I want to tell you more about Jess.
    I can't tell you how old Jess was. He always seemed old, and he never seemed to change. He was Old Jess Potter when I was five, and he was Old Jess Potter when I was sixteen, and he was Old Jess Potter when he died thirty years or so ago. And I don't know where Jess Potter originated, nor does anyone else. Apparently he just appeared in Smalltown one day around 1900. There always was speculation that he was the retarded child of a wealthy family who had visited the area and who left him behind as people do with unwanted dogs and cats. Others say he walked off a visiting schooner and never got back on board. Still others say he was the leader of one of the wandering religious sects that came to the Cape to see the end of the world, and that when the prophecy was proven false, he went blank and never recovered all of his senses. And then there was Dr. Hall's explanation.
    Whatever his origins, by my earliest time he was a fixture in town. No one ever called him Jess or Mr. Potter; he was always Jess Potter, whether you spoke to him or about him.
    He always appeared aged, always wore the same clothing, and always was smiling. Yet he didn't smell or anything like that. In fact, both he and his clothing always smelled of soap. I expect that he had always taken a lot of abusive teasing, but I have no recollection of anyone ever being mad or angry or insulting with him, even when he did exasperating things. People would, and with certain justification, become frustrated because of something Jess Potter did or didn't do, but they never took it out on him directly.
    Jess Potter was our town character, a unique, one-of-a-kind institution, almost, and we loved him. He was incapable of meanness. Dull-witted, uneducated, slow, he also was caring, sensitive and anything but lazy.

Robert Wolley

Jess Potter's world was black and white. If he didn't like something or someone, he would shake his head slowly from side to side and whisper, "That's a no; that's a no go; that's a no go, Moe." It never varied.

Frank asked him once who Moe was. "That's me middle name," he answered, "Jessup Moe Potter."

"So what do ya mean when ya say 'no go, Moe'?"

"I's tellin' me whole self 'That's a no; that's a no go'."

Frank let it go at that.

Women gave Jess Potter a little room because of his habit of expressing his like for something. He'd start a whistle, break it off to shout "She's a beaut!", take his index finger and draw circles around his ear, and then point to the object of his liking, whether it was a pretty girl or a car or a dog or boat. I must say he had an obvious like for some of the summer people's daughters and automobiles, which may help account for the women's reaction.

I'm quick to add that never once did he do anything other than that to warrant the least bit of apprehension or suspicion about his attention to beauty.

Thus to Dr. Hall's evidence and theory, and since Jess Potter had a room with the Halls and had ever since coming to Smalltown, I tend to give Dr. Hall's explanation credence.

Dr. Hall had let it be known, according to Aunt Hattie, that before Jess Potter came to Smalltown he had been gelded somewhere in Africa by captors who had seized his ship.

Whatever else was taken, it was obvious to Frank and me that Jess Potter had also lost some of his brain. So when it was our turn to hear of the castration part, we figured there was a sly way to learn more. We asked Miss Barney, one of our teachers, if you could take part of a man's brains like they took another of Jess Potter's parts. She got all red in the face and said she'd wash out our mouths with soap if we ever dared to ask another question like that.

The Pranks An' Enlightenment of Frank An' Me

That struck us as sort of strange. People had horses and everyone seemed to know about "fixin'" them. We used to go to the fish hatchery in Sayersville and watch female fish being stripped and male fish being milked, so we had some vague idea about reproduction. We had expected a straight answer to a serious question. Miss Barney wasn't any help whatsoever.

But she did raise our interest. Frank didn't want to, but I knew that his pa read a lot, so I asked him about taking part of a man's brain. He told us about hospitals that took out part of the front of the brain to make people behave better. Lop something or other he called it.

I did so well with that question that I ventured the other operation. Lordy, he got agitated too, said I should be asking my pa, which, of course, I couldn't because Pa had left long before.

But then Frank's pa began talking about some woman named Esther from the Bible and about men called chamberlains, and I couldn't make head nor tail of it except that sometimes men were operated on to serve God's purposes.

After that, Frank and I did what anyone would do. We looked Jess Potter's head all over for signs of an operation, and we waited for Jess Potter to do something for God.

Jess Potter did all kinds of odd jobs, usually unpleasant ones, all over town. Gran'ma would hire him sometimes if Pa didn't fix something as quickly as Gran'ma wanted. Jess Potter sometimes was good at mechanical things, provided that they were straightforward and could be done one step at a time.

One day Ma discovered that the Model A had a flat tire. It was before Pa left home, but he was off somewhere, so Ma said to get Jess Potter who was working at Cole's Inn.

Sure enough, before long he came, happy as always. He pitched right in. He jacked up the rear end of the Model A, took off the tire, and patched it. How much, Ma asked? Twenty five cents, Jess Potter said. Not enough, Gran'ma said. A dollar, he said, and that would include cleaning the car inside and out. Ma said a dollar if he'd scrub the top.

The deal was set, with Ma's instruction that the washing of the car be done in the shade and the top scrubbing be done out where the sun would dry the canvas.

Since he always finished every job, there was no reason to check on Jess Potter, but after a couple of hours, when he didn't come to the door for his money, Ma sent me out. Jess Potter had half the engine on the ground.

"What ya up to, Jess Potter?" I asked.

"I'm fixin' 'er," he said. "Couldn't get the beaut to move. Must be the clutch."

I didn't know anything about that, so I told Ma that Jess Potter was fixing something that was wrong. She gave a shout when she saw the mess. "Go up an' have Aunt Hattie call Crane's," she hollered at me.

Aunt Hattie's was about a mile and a half, so it took a little while. Then there was the usual jawing with Aunt Hattie, her ever present need to leave her post at the switchboard to go to the necessary, her searching for a few pennies to pay me for tending to calls, of which there were none, and finally the call to Crane's, and then the walk home.

I was gone for over an hour, and during that time more of the engine had been left on the ground. Jess Potter was determined, if nothing else.

Late in the day, two of Crane's men showed up. In his unique way, Jess Potter explained that the automobile wouldn't move when he started it up.

Thank the Lord that Jess was a slow worker. He could have had every nut and bolt on the ground, but as it was it took the two Crane men almost two hours to get everything back together. And, sure enough, when they cranked up the Ford, it sounded fine but wouldn't move.

The Pranks An' Enlightenment of Frank An' Me

It was decided to leave it until morning when the men could see what they were doing.

At first light, and I mean before sunup, there was a knock on the kitchen door. It was Jess Potter, ready to lend a hand. It would be at least three hours before Crane's men came, but Jess Potter just settled in on one of the settees in the back yard.

Pa had gotten home late, so he was upset, first by being awakened. Then he was upset because his automobile was broken. Then he was upset because Ma had hired Jess Potter for a whole dollar. And he was upset because Jess Potter had just been invited to breakfast by Gran'ma. And he was even more upset when Gran'ma preached a little about Christian charity. When Jess Potter came into the house wearing his ever-present smile, Pa hit the roof and went back to bed.

And Ma was upset when I allowed as how I could miss a day of school to witness whatever there was to be seen. "Sonny," she growled, "'bout now I'd like nothin' better than ta tan someone's hide. 'Nother word an' it's agoin' ta be yours."

When I got home, Pa had his right foot in a bucket of ice. It seems that when Crane's men finally got there, Pa was still in bed. He went out in his bare feet, and when the Model A wouldn't move, he applied the only remedy he knew. He kicked it. Dr. Hall said he broke his big toe.

Crane's men finally had to give up and said they'd tow the automobile to the garage where they would work on it.

Jess Potter listened quietly. He had hung around all day, getting a free breakfast and lunch. When the talk of towing was raised, he volunteered. "Jess Potter will help. Just let me take the jacks out from under the rear end."

There was a deathly silence. Gran'ma stepped between Jess Potter and Pa. "No, you don't!" she yelled at Pa. "No one's goin', ta touch 'im."

Jess Potter didn't even realize what he had done, and Pa being mad didn't even get to him. All he said was, "I'm goin' ta wash it soon's it's comes back," pleased with the prospect of another day's work. "I 'ready changed the tire an' swept her out. Maybe you'll pay me for that now."

No one would take Jess Potter on a boat. He was limited to small jobs and running errands. And you only let him run an errand if time meant nothing.

One day Frank and I were on the beach with my skiff. We wanted to turn it over and scrape the bottom. Barnacles and grass had taken a good hold of the bottom. As we were struggling to lift the boat and turn it over, along came Jess Potter. "Need a hand?" he asks. We tell him yes. "Can't help but a minute," he says. "Have to git this here package o' net weights to Mr. Pierson."

We'd seen Mr. Pierson earlier. He seemed in a hurry to get his boat away, said that he had heard of a late run of mackerel and hoped to find it.

Probably Jess Potter's package was a last-minute addition. But a minute's help would be appreciated.

When we got the skiff over, the amount of growth was considerable. Usually, we'd knock off the barnacles with stones and wash the bottom with sand, just using our hands. But Jess Potter convinced us that we needed a scraper and a heavy wire brush. "I know just where they be on the wharf," he offered, "an' I'll get 'em."

He took off on the run. We figured he'd deliver Mr. Pierson's weights, Mr. Pierson's boat being tied to the far end of the pier. We didn't pay any attention to the package when Jess Potter returned with two scrapers and a wire brush.

He helped get the bottom as smooth as glass. Then he helped turn the skiff over and drag it to the water. We all rowed over to the wharf.

"Got ta return them tools," Jess Potter told us. "Always be sure ta return what ya borrow 'cause ya welcome ta borrow

The Pranks An' Enlightenment of Frank An' Me

'gain." He was right about that. "An' clean. Always take 'em back cleaner than when ya got 'em."

He had his arms full when he climbed the ladder. "Look," whispered Frank, "he's still got Mr. Pierson's weights." Sure enough, the package was as yet undelivered.

"Jess Potter," Frank called, "did you forget something?"

"No," Jess Potter answered. "I got two scrapers, one wire brush, an' Mr. Pierson's box."

We climbed the ladder. Mr. Pierson's fishing boat was long gone. Probably Mr. Pierson gave up waiting for whoever was delivering his seine weights. Chances are, if he had known Jess Potter was the deliverer, Mr. Pierson would have gone after them himself.

"Well, that's not nice," Jess Potter told us when there was no boat waiting. "Here I got Mr. Pierson's box. Rushed all the way from Peterson's to get it ta 'im, an' he don't wait. It's a no; it's a no go; it's a no go, Moe."

Jess Potter liked to pump the organ in the Methodist church. His efforts were not always appreciated because he found the pumping too strenuous at times and often would stop to wipe his forehead, at which point the organ always *whooshed* out of breath and Jess Potter always said the same thing, "Suck in some air, you fool!" And always loud enough to be heard by the congregation.

I don't think Jess Potter ever made the connection between the pumping and the air. I think he thought he made the music, not the air flow that became the music through the organist's fingers on the keys that opened the leathers on the pipes. I say this because if the music was particularly stirring, Jess Potter would step out onto the chancel floor and take a bow.

I was maybe fourteen when I came right out and asked Dr. Hall whether Jess Potter had had an operation on his brain. Frank and I had been wondering that for years, I said.

"Well," he answered, "I've heard that suggested before, but it ain't so. Jessup has everything the good Lord gave him, and it ain't much."

When I giggled, he added, "Well, that ain't quite true, is it. I suppose you know it ain't."

When I allowed as much, confessing to Dr. Hall at the same time that I didn't know more than the horrible things I heard, he said, "Well, son, it's true."

I asked a lot of hows and whys and what Dr. Hall told me went something like this. Jess Potter had been a seaman, probably not too bright, Dr. Hall figured, but strong and willing. He had sailed to north Africa as a boy, sometime in the years after the Civil War, on a trader of some kind maybe, maybe even a smuggling ship.

As near as Dr. Hall could figure it, some kind of fight took place, Jess Potter's ship was captured, and he was put or sold into slavery. Dr. Hall guessed that being young, strong and sort of dumb, Jess Potter was sold to some African chief with lots of wives and that the wives needed to be guarded and that Jess Potter fit the bill, so he was "fixed" not to have ideas about the African's women.

But, said Dr. Hall, he had no idea how Jess Potter escaped or how he came back to America or how or why he ended up in Smalltown, only that he did.

One day, according to Dr. Hall, when he was just starting his practice in Smalltown, Jess Potter came to his house. He didn't go to the door and knock; he just took down the doc's new sign and sat on the front steps holding it. Actually, one of the patients came across Jess Potter and told the doc about him.

"I went out, and sure enough there be this sickly fellow. I asked him what he wanted. He didn't say nothing, just pointed to the sign and then to me. First I figured he couldn't talk. I took him into the house. Of course, then I lived alone, not yet married. Well, I had a patient to tend, so I left the fellow in the

The Pranks An' Enlightenment of Frank An' Me

waiting room. When I finished with the patient, no one was there, but the room had been picked up."

Dr. Hall went on to say that he found the man, Jessup Potter, cleaning up the doc's kitchen. To make a long story short, Jess Potter was sick but mostly from malnutrition. Doc examined him, and that's when he discovered the wicked thing that had been done.

"Once I saw that," Dr. Hall went on, "and maybe because I didn't run away or kick the man out, he told me his name and what little I've told you. I never learned a single bit more. I fed Jessup and gave him some medicine and right then I took a liking to him and he's been living with me ever since. He is a fine man, if you have tolerance for someone different."

Dr. Hall contacted the Seaman's Union and hiring halls and shelters all over. No one had ever heard of Jessup Moe Potter. Dr. Hall's guess, and he said it was only a guess, was that Jess Potter was an orphan, and that when he got to be twelve or thirteen, whoever was caring for him gave him to a ship captain. He belonged to no one, so no one ever missed him. He'd never learned to read or write but had learned to make his initials, JMP.

Jess Potter was in the doc's house when Dr. Hall took his bride there, had helped take care of the Hall children, and had assisted the doctor sometimes with things like broken bones and cuts. "He has more, far more, than earned his way," Doc said. "Took care of my horses and carriage before I had an automobile. Did all the cleaning and cooking for Mrs. Hall. Took care of Mrs. Hall when she was sick. Nursed her right up to the day she died. Better than I could. And he still takes care of me."

I had a new appreciation of Jess Potter, and I think Frank did too when I told him all that Dr. Hall had said.

"One more thing," Dr. Hall said to me. "I want to tell you one more thing about Jessup. Folks give him respect because they see under all his slowness and sometimes foolish behavior, a great heart. Jessup wasn't favored much in the brain department and he was hurt more than most men ever could be by other men. He ain't never complained, never said one word that was bad. On the contrary, he's done some wonderful things to help people, things that most people never have known."

If you remember, I told you about Grace Willis and her house being burned to the ground and about Jess Potter throwing out from the second floor all the breakable things. Dr. Hall told me more.

Jess Potter, it seems, was terribly upset because he hadn't been able to save the house. He blamed himself because Grace Willis lost her home. So, after the fire, he cleaned up the whole mess all by himself and fixed up the foundation, getting it ready for a new house.

Then he went to Pilot and Sayersville and Northam and wherever there was a barn falling down, asked if he could have the lumber, and then carried it to Smalltown and to the widow Willis's place. It took him months. I used to see him carrying boards and wondered what he was building.

He cleaned up the boards and even trued up the heavy timbers. Dr. Hall didn't know where he had learned that skill or how he had managed to carry some of the great timbers, but he did. He stacked everything in neat piles.

Only after he had done all that, he told Dr. Hall that he wanted to build a house but didn't know how.

Dr. Hall assumed that Jess Potter wanted to build a house for himself and asked how it was going to be paid for and where the land was and all that. Jess Potter said he would show the doctor and took him to the Willis place. Jess Potter didn't want a place for himself but for poor Grace Willis, she being so much worse off than he was.

Doc said he cried right there. "I thought," he said, "that

The Pranks An' Enlightenment of Frank An' Me

maybe I was looking at God. Least at God's finest work. That night I thanked the Lord for sending Jessup to us."

When Jess Potter died, he had been alone for several years. Dr. Hall had died and in his will had left the house and some money to take care of it to Jessup Moe Potter for, the will read, "to take care of this friend of God, my friend and teacher, who showed me what humanity could be, the true 'beaut' of Smalltown, for as long as he shall live."

Dr. Hall's house is now the Smalltown Historical Society building, given to the town by the Hall children. When you walk in, there's an oversized picture of the Halls with their children when the children had grown some. Standing behind the children is Jess Potter. It's not a formal picture; everyone is smiling. The biggest smile is Jess Potter's.

Robert Wolley

Chapter XII

The Fine Arts

The Pranks An' Enlightenment of Frank An' Me

I should tell you about Paul Abbey and what happened to him and about the Chambers girls. In a way Mr. Abbey and the Chambers girls were related, not by marriage or blood or anything like that but by the way certain things worked out.

Mr. Abbey and Alice Hargood brought notice to the town with their antics, and when Mr. Abbey returned, he brought us a little more excitement and spice.

The Chambers girls were a part of that, although quite innocently, and, well, let me tell it this way.

On beautiful summer days around Smalltown, the beaches and dunes were covered with men and women, mostly women, wearing straw hats, sitting on camp stools, painting pictures of everything in sight.

I didn't know anything about art, still don't, and neither did Frank, but every opportunity we'd get, we'd take time to look at the paintings when the artists were about. We started doing that when we were eight or nine, and by the time we were thirteen or fourteen, we had developed quite a routine.

We'd walk up behind the artist, one of us on either shoulder, and just stand there. Then we'd start to cough a little and do a bit of tongue noise, disapproving of the painting. Then one of us would say something like, "I liked Mr. Jones's dunes better," or "Miss Brown knew how to draw the boats."

That always got the painter's attention. Then we would back off without talking to the painter and go to a spot somewhere close by where we would make a production out of smoothing out the sand. One of us would make some meaningless lines while the other pointed first to the painter and then to the spot in the sand. That usually got them.

It took a really self-controlled painter to not at least try to see what we had scratched. If one ever got up to come and look, we'd rub our nonsense lines out and walk away, shaking our heads. More than one painter actually shouted for us to come and show her how to improve her painting. Imagine asking a couple of art-ignorant boys for guidance. We took that as the highest praise for our little joke.

Actually, I had one accomplishment that might have been helpful. I could draw boats, the lines and the proper perspective. Lots of artists had trouble in that area, and more than one dory ended up looking like a kitchen table. Few, however, were inclined to take a boy's advice.

Frank was quite good drawing marsh grasses and the little flowers that grew in the protected lee of the dunes. His secret, which I wished more artists had discovered, was the simplicity of the stems and leaves and flowers. His drawings were like those of the Chinese and Japanese screens and pottery found in the Cape homes of earlier China-trade sailors. Less was better.

One day we were just getting into our routine with a gentleman painter when Frank gave me a poke. If I didn't sense it, Frank did. The man was no amateur.

He put his brushes down. "You damn kids going to say anything?" he asked.

"It's wonderful," Frank answered with obvious regard for the painting. Then, I thought, he went and spoiled it by adding, "What is it?"

The man stood up. "You like it and you don't even know what you're seeing. That's kind of dumb, don't you think?"

Frank didn't bat an eyelash. "Lots of beautiful things I've seen that I don't know what they are."

"Jesus," shouted the man, "you're a damn politician, or a philosopher. Look at it."

The painting was wild, with lots of colors and splashes. But the man wasn't paying any attention to me. He was pressing Frank. "What beautiful things have you seen that you can't tell me what they are?"

Frank took a deep breath. "Sunrise and sunset for two," he answered defiantly. "And the northern lights. And sometimes when I look at my mother, and ...."

The Pranks An' Enlightenment of Frank An' Me

"Okay, okay. I've asked a stupid question and you've given me an artist's answer, and a damn good one to boot. Now look at the painting. You have responded to the whole thing without seeing it. Look at it again and tell me what you see."

"The ocean and the sky, and sails. But I ain't never seen yellow and purple and black sails. And I ain't never seen a green sky or a red sea or boats up in the sky."

Pointing out over the water, the man said something about that being how he saw it. "We're all sailing, son, and the red sea represents our blood, or at least mankind's blood, and the sails are different colors because we're all different colors, and the sky's green because even if we evolved from the sea we all cling to the earth, the good green earth. That's one explanation."

"There's more?" I piped up.

"Oh, yes. I could tell you that we're all sailing alone just as peacefully as can be but that among us is that black sail. And black is death, and evil, and doom. And I could tell you that some of us are sailing free, see the sails in the sky, but that's not what I mean. Some of us are lost; that's what I want you to see."

It was an education, to say the least, most of it lost on me but none of it lost on Frank, especially when the man was telling Frank about impressions and abstractions. We never had met a real artist before that seemed truly delighted in talking with us and explaining his painting, probably because we had never seen anything like this painting before.

Frank nearly jumped out of his shoes when the man put up a piece of white board and told Frank to paint his own picture.

When Frank asked what he should paint, the man said for him to look around, find something that he liked or that meant something or was just plain interesting, and put it on the board.

Frank did a surprising thing. He turned his back on the water. "Most of all, I like them low green hills with the oaks and pines. when we're out on the water, I always feel better when them hills and trees come into view."

Robert Wolley

"Good," the man said. "Close your eyes for a minute and try to see the hills as you first see them when you're coming back from fishing or wherever you've been. Then sketch them with this brush." He handed Frank a paint brush and guided his hand into some yellow paint. "Use a light color; you can always paint over it. Just outline the hills lightly."

The lesson went on for some time, and I lost interest until the man shouted, "Look what you've done! You've gone and painted your mother's breasts. Look at those two hills." He laughed and teased Frank.

Frank turned as red as a beet. "No, no, son," the man reassured Frank. "It's nothing to get embarrassed about. Forget that I mentioned your mother; think of it as mother earth. You are painting your security, not very well I must admit, but you'll get the hang of it if you take lessons and practice."

The man insisted that Frank work some on the painting, but Frank didn't seem to want to. The artist then sat Frank down, asking if he could be forgiven for his reference to Frank's mother.

Frank had no choice. Then the man did another surprising thing. "Look at this," he said. "I'll paint what I think you were trying to express. And as you might have done it."

He painted swiftly, following the two hills Frank had marked, working them into dunes and making a terrible jagged line between them and the water. The hills and dunes were handsome, but the water was made to boil and looked threatening. The black line between the two spoiled both. As soon as he started to paint that line I hated the picture.

"Is that the idea?"

Frank shook his head.

"You want the painting?"

Again Frank shook his head.

The Pranks An' Enlightenment of Frank An' Me

"I've gone too far, haven't I?" The man looked at Frank. "Sometimes I paint things that I didn't even know were in my mind."

Then Frank did a surprising thing. First he asked the man what the man thought was in Frank's mind and then he asked the man to paint those thoughts in the artist's own way.

"Well," the man said thoughtfully, "you suggested a conflict. I assumed the conflict was between a certain fear, or should I say respect, for the dangers of the ocean and the security of the land. Perhaps I assumed too much. Perhaps there's a conflict between home and wanting to be somewhere else, or maybe between being the fisherman you're going to be and wanting to be something else."

"I don't know." That's all Frank said. "I don't know."

The man continued. "I'm remembering when I was a boy. I always wanted things to stay just as they were. I liked being a boy; in fact, I never wanted to grow up. Now I'm an artist and some people say I never have grown up, still live in a world of dreams and images."

All the time the man was talking, he was painting. He went over the hills with great splotches of color. Up close they were a mess, but a few feet away they were a magnificent fall scene, with light seeming to pour in from every angle. The ocean sparkled and seemed to hug the shore with little hands and fingers. That kind of art I could understand. It was when he started to paint the fog standing off shore that I became uncomfortable.

"Fog is the hardest thing in the world to paint," he said. "Ask any artist."

The fog was menacing. That's what I remember now, just how threatening the fog appeared and how it seemed as though it would engulf everything as it rolled in.

When the man put down his brushes, Frank said, "Yes. That's how I feel. There is something that scares me, makes me feel uneasy."

Then the man did his last surprising thing. He took a putty knife and began scraping away all of the paint. 'There is always some kind of apprehension hanging over us," he explained. "I don't like to paint it, even if it is a fact of life. Focus too much on the unnamed fears and all we'll do is spend our lives frightened by every shadow."

Frank never did say much about that day. He was upset on the one hand that the man had found the breast image and that he had exposed some worrying image within Frank. On the other hand he had been enlightened that everything could be seen in one's own way, no matter how it looked to someone else.

Now, I put an adult's interpretation on that day, an adult with experience. We had no experience, to say the least, and certainly would not have used such words an enlightened and image and interpretation. Such are my words today. But wordless, Frank was visibly changed by that experience.

If he ever did take up painting, I didn't know of it, but from that day he seemed to see things differently, which is one of the reasons he could come up with such great ideas.

As artists became more numerous, and a few studios and galleries opened, the Cape became one great big art colony with sizable canvases taking the place of a lot of pictures that used to be painted on the inside of shells. I guess there were always serious artists on the Cape, but suddenly there were hundreds of them.

Enter Paul Abbey. One day posters appeared all over Smalltown advertising a new art gallery. Frank saw the posters first and for some reason got real excited. He came to the house to get me; he wanted me to see the posters. Remember the man

The Pranks An' Enlightenment of Frank An' Me

who let me paint, he asked? He was so excited, jumping up and down, that I just had to follow him.

The posters were in black and white, and the picture was hard to make out, if there was a picture at all. "Look," Frank yelled in my ear, "Look at that!"

I didn't have the heart to tell him that I couldn't see anything but a mess of black splotches. It wouldn't have mattered anyway, with Frank carrying on about the beauty of it all. I looked, but instead of studying the painting that was supposedly there, I read the script. It mentioned a new gallery for artists. I remember the words to this day, "who paint in a new, freer style."

And who was the owner of the new gallery? None other than Mr. Paul Abbey who, the posters said, had "returned from around the world of art" to bring new art to Smalltown.

The posters went on to invite "artists who dare to paint in new ways" to place their art in the gallery and to invite people to come and look and, I supposed, to buy.

Frank had not bothered to read the poster. He saw only the word "gallery" and the painting and was dumbfounded when I put my finger on Mr. Abbey's name.

Neither of us had known that Mr. Abbey had returned from wherever he had gone. That night I found out that neither Ma nor Gran'ma knew either, and of course that meant that Aunt Hattie hadn't known; if she didn't know, then no one did. The posters were the first anyone knew.

Right off, after reading the poster, Frank and I went to the gallery on Chessman Street, a little alley off Depot Avenue, just off Main Street. A sign on the door said "To be opened." No date or anything, not even the word "soon."

I did learn from Aunt Hattie that a telephone had been ordered for the building but not under Paul Abbey's name. The name was Warren Chambers! He was the Chambers' girls' father.

Warren Chambers was a jack-of-all-trades, and from what people said, he was the master of all the trades he practiced: carpenter, electrician, mechanic, typesetter. That last was a little unusual for Smalltown, perhaps, but I guess he did print cards and stationery in a little shop in his barn, but not enough to make a living.

Mr. Chambers was away some because he took jobs wherever he could find them. But he was always was at home on the weekends, though, because he was an usher in the Methodist church on Sundays, even if Mrs. Chambers and the girls did go to the Catholic church.

Among other things he did, Mr. Chambers had been making picture frames in his barn for a lot of the artists. I learned that he had been hired by Mr. Abbey to renovate the house on Chessman Street into a gallery on the condition that no one was to know for whom he was working. Mr. Abbey had bought the house, but the deed wasn't transferred until the day the posters appeared. Mr. Chambers had signed for the telephone because Mr. Abbey had asked him to do so as part of the renovation. Later, the telephone was reassigned to Mr. Abbey. The house had been owned by the town for years, having been taken for taxes many years before.

I'm not certain now how I learned all this or in what order; it doesn't matter much. What did matter was that Mr. Abbey was back in town and that he was going to open a gallery which promised new and different art. That part got Frank excited.

One day, the gallery still closed but promising "to be opened," I saw Mr. Abbey coming out of the post office. Rather, he saw me first. "Well, laddie, still catchin' them minnows?" he asked. "You've grown some. How's your mother?" He didn't stop talking and said goodbye before I had a chance to say anything.

That night, a little after supper, there was a knock on the back door. I went to answer it. There stood Mr. Abbey.

The Pranks An' Enlightenment of Frank An' Me

Now mind you, I liked Mr. Abbey. He always had been kind to Frank and me, generous in seeing that we had bait for our minnow nets, including us in his automobile jaunts, and giving a more than fair measure to Ma and Gran'ma when they bought meat. Even if the stories about his days before coming to Smalltown were true, he had lived them down.

But the rumrunning business and his doings with Alice Hargood had discolored all that. When he drifted away and didn't come back, like everybody else, I guess I figured too bad but good riddance.

Now here he was, his ample frame filling the entire doorway, asking for Ma.

I don't remember the exact conversation, but it went something like this:

"Ev'nin', ma'am."

"Ev'nin', Mr. Abbey."

"Have you been well?"

"Yes, thank you, Mr. Abbey."

"Would you be invitin' me into your house?"

"I don't think so, Mr. Abbey."

When Ma said that, she reached over and put her arm around my shoulder. She'd never done that in her life. I figured it was a signal, nothing to do with affection and everything to do with protection. But at the moment I couldn't figure from what. Paul Abbey had never been more than a casual friend to Ma. Was he seeking more? Was that what was worrying Ma?

"Perhaps this isn't a good time. Could I call on you at a more appropriate time?"

When Ma hesitated, he asked if tomorrow afternoon, say two o'clock, would be a good time. I could sense that Ma knew right well that she would have to talk with Paul Abbey eventually. She agreed.

Gran'ma, of course, had heard every word. "Well, well, well," she muttered. "Ain't wastin' no time, that gamecock."

Ma was silent.

I went to bed soon after that but couldn't sleep, speculating on so many things, jumping to all kinds of conclusions. I heard Ma and Gran'ma talking. Usually I would have listened; that's how I got to know some of the things I did. But that night my own imagination blocked out the voices. I imagined all sorts of things, scenes and events, but the one thing I couldn't imagine was having Paul Abbey as my pa.

The next morning I was torn about what I would or should do. I was supposed to help Mr. Peterson, doing some stock moving in the morning, and Mr. Prince was giving me some afternoon work making boxes for his oysters, and that night I'd go down to the scallop docks to see if there'd be any work the next day, in case someone's crew was sick or something.

If I kept all of my agreements, I'd miss Mr. Abbey's visit completely. Ma sensed my dilemma when I didn't rush off to Peterson's. "Okay, boy," she said, "off ya go. Ain't goin' ta be nothin' here for ya anyway."

When I protested, Ma said, "If there's somethin' ya should know, though I can't for the life of me imagine what that be, I'll tell ya. Get 'long now. This be adult business."

Getting shoved out of my own house with so little ceremony got me to imagining even more. So I did what was natural. I made a beeline to Frank's house, told him what had been done, and in the best dramatic mode of the comic books we read, asked him to keep an eye on my house and on Mr. Abbey.

"But I'm deliverin' for Mr. Beers," Frank protested.

I registered disappointment but said I understood.

"But," Frank said, "it's a perfect cover. All us spies need a cover. I'll do it. Have a full report for ya tonight."

Every delivery Frank made that day went near, by or around my house. Mr. Beers got real angry at Frank because each delivery took so long, accusing Frank of running up the time.

The Pranks An' Enlightenment of Frank An' Me

Frank took one of his school notebooks and recorded every look: the time, what he saw, which usually was exactly nothing, how long he spent looking. He even drew little maps showing the house and with little Xs marking his spying places. He had borrowed his pa's binoculars, so some of his spying places were unique, to say the least.

But I was interested only in the two o'clock sighting.

At Peterson's I noticed some boxes originally marked with Mr. Chambers' name but with that crossed out and Mr. Abbey's name written over. When I mentioned it to Mr. Peterson, he said it was some kind of surprise that Mr. Abbey had returned to Smalltown and another kind of surprise that he was opening an art gallery. The boxes contained artists' supplies.

I asked Mr. Peterson where he figured Mr. Abbey had been for the past couple of years. He said he didn't know, and I was sure he didn't. Then I allowed as how Mr. Abbey must have learned something about painting. Mr. Peterson gave a little chuckle and said that he didn't think Mr. Abbey knew anything about art or about running an art gallery.

It was obvious that there was nothing to be learned from that conversation, so I let it drop. Mr. Peterson was more in the dark than I was.

And Mr. Prince, when I finally got to his barn, knew even less, only that someone had told him what I've already reported. Mr. Prince, though, was very sparse with words, and all afternoon I wondered if he did know something that he was not telling.

Mr. Prince had accumulated a great scrap of lumber. He cut and split the necessary pieces and I nailed the pieces into boxes on a frame he said had come from his gran'pa so all the boxes would be the same size for good packing.

"Ya gran'pa had an eye," he said at one point. "Could measure by eye, bevel a lapstrake by eye. God gave him a talent for seein'."

Then he asked, "Did ya know that a few times men come down from Boston jest ta try ta git 'im ta go up there an' help make pianos?" I hadn't known that.

"Or that men come from as far as New York jest ta git him ta make special planin' tools?" I hadn't known that either.

"So why didn't he go to Boston?"

"Don't know. But I tell ya this, as good as his eye was with a piece of timber, his eye for men were even better." And Mr. Prince added the opening I thought might be there. "He'd have figured out Paul Abbey in a minute."

"But what's ta figure?"

"Whether Abbey's up ta somethin'."

At that point I told Mr. Prince about Paul Abbey's visit the previous night and his planned visit that very afternoon and about my speculating.

"Well, I could tell ya ta go home, but ya ma'd be right mad. Whatever it is is 'tween her an' Abbey. She'll do right, an' ya gran'ma'll see ta that. She is a right smart woman, ya gran'ma, like ya gran'pa. I does think, though, ya're imaginin' thin's what ain't likely."

That was a long speech for Mr. Prince. He slowed down his cutting and I could see that he was speculating, just like I'd been doing.

At last he said, "Lad, any man here'd be proud ta have ya for a son. Lord knows ya pa got sidetracked, but ya, an' Frank, too, is good boys. Don't be feared ta ask for help if the time comes." Mr. Prince looked directly into my eyes. "I mean it, lad. Ya're most of what we got fer tomorrow."

I already knew how much people cared, and sometimes it was like carrying a pocketful of net weights, knowing that, and trying not to disappoint them. I didn't say anything, just nodded

The Pranks An' Enlightenment of Frank An' Me

my head. Mr. Prince knew well enough that I heard and understood.

All of a sudden he shouted "Lord Almighty, I've been carryin' on. Talk too much an' do the work o' the devil, they say." And except for a word here and there, that was the end of conversation for the day.

About four o'clock we quit. Mr. Prince gave me a dollar, way too much for the few hours of work. And Mr. Peterson had given me fifty cents for almost four hours, which considering he also gave me a couple of birch beers and some candy, was way more than fair.

I rushed home, my curiosity bursting beyond belief, only before I got home I got waylaid by Frank. He pulled me into the orchard behind Cole's Inn.

"Sure no one's followed ya?" he began. "Let's get out of sight — got to be careful." He made a full sweep of the area with his pa's glass.

Satisfied, he handed me his notebook. "Here. It's all down. Read it, memorize it, eat it."

And while I was reading his notes and admiring his drawings, he slipped away. I didn't even hear him leave.

There were no revelations, just observations. One was that Mr. Abbey walked to see Ma. No automobile. Frank noted that that was uncharacteristic of Mr. Abbey's former life style. Another was that Mr. Abbey arrived early at the end of the alley, checked his watch frequently, and timed his knock precisely at two. He stayed exactly twenty-two minutes. When he left, Frank followed him toward town but had to break off when he got to Beers's.

There was a note about Mr. Beers being upset and that Frank had told Mr. Beers that I would explain why Frank was late all day. The note also said that Mr. Beers wasn't going to pay Frank for a full day's work, so I owed Frank some money.

Fat chance, I said to myself, but I did feel a little guilty, wondering how I was going to get Frank off the hook.

There was no one home, and there was no note. Ma seldom left notes unless she wanted an errand run or someone would be giving me a little work. I couldn't seem to get my mind focused on anything, so I rummaged around for something to eat. I still had it in mind to try for a berth on one of the scallop boats. Actually, that's what Ma expected me to do since I had told her that, so maybe she didn't expect me to show up for more than a few minutes. On the other hand, she knew full well that I was chock full of curiosity and interest in what Mr. Abbey might be proposing.

No Ma and no Gran'ma for the longest time. It wasn't like them to stay away before suppertime except when the ladies met at Aunt Hattie's, and that wasn't today. As a matter of fact, the ladies' gatherings were almost at an end, what with Aunt Hattie fixing to get married.

That marriage was a lot longer coming than was supposed, for reasons I won't go into here other than to say that the planned fancy telephone exchange was way behind and that Aunt Hattie was still plugging in the lines.

I decided that being idle was not good, so I elected to drop down to Mr. Beers's place. With pay burning a hole in my pocket, I could get a birch beer or a cream soda. For the moment I had forgotten what Frank had written about my needing to explain to Mr. Beers why Frank was so behind all day.

There was no one in the store when I got my bottle of cream soda. I went out back to give Mr. Beers his nickel.

"What ya do ta Frank?" was Mr. Beers' first words. "Every time he went out of here he was gone for hours. Said he was helpin' ya an' ya ma. But ya ma were here not long ago an' she said she ain't seen Frank all day an' you be workin' for Prince."

"Well," I started, but I couldn't continue. Mr. Beers had never forgiven Mr. Abbey for wrecking the store.

The Pranks An' Enlightenment of Frank An' Me

"You boys been up ta somethin'; I can tell jest by lookin' at ya. Now, ain't none of my business, but 'tis when I promise my customers delivery an' them deliveries are way late."

"Mr. Beers," I said, "I 'pologize for Frank. He were doin' somethin' terrible 'portant fer me. Not my Ma; she knowed nothin' 'bout it. I'd rather not say what it was. But blame me, not Frank."

"You in trouble?"

"No, I ain't. Nothin' like that."

"Well, I got no right ta ask ya," and Mr. Beers let the whole matter drop right there. He would know soon enough if Frank and I were in trouble.

Ma was home when I got back. "Well?" I asked. "What Mr. Abbey have ta say fer hisself?"

"Nothin'."

"Nothing! He spent twenty-two minutes here an' didn't say nothin?"

"I ain't sayin' an' that's the end of it. I don't want ta hear any more questions."

I could tell that Ma was upset. Whatever had gone on must have been unpleasant. But what went on? That's what I wanted to know.

Ma had turned her back to me. Suddenly she spun around. "How do ya know how long Mr. Abbey were here?" she demanded.

"I don't know. Jest a guess."

"You spyin' on me?"

"No, Ma. I was with Mr. Prince all afternoon."

"Frank! You had Frank doin' your spyin'. Now I know what Mr. Beers were talkin' 'bout. My own son, gettin' someone else ta do his dirty spyin'."

"Ma. What you an' Mr. Abbey plan has to do with me. Did he ask ta marry ya?"

"Good Lord Almighty! Do ya think I'd be marryin' 'im? Lord Almighty!"

"Did he ask?"

"No, he didn't. Nothin' like that. Weren't nothin' like that. It were business. Oh, for goodness sakes, jest let it drop."

I had to, I guess, at least for a time. But what in the world could Mr. Abbey have proposed that would have been so upsetting? I was getting no help at home, but I would find out. No secret in Smalltown could be secret forever. One particular thing I wanted to know was if Paul Abbey had insulted Ma. I was getting downright angry, but I didn't have the slightest reason why.

For the first time, I had something I couldn't share, not even with Frank. Maybe that's why I gave him fifty cents when I returned his notebook the next morning.

"I weren't no help?" he asked.

"Ya did fine."

"Is that all ya're goin' ta say?"

"Yah. Can't say more."

"Can I ask if you're goin' to have a new pa?"

"Can ask, an' I ain't."

Good old Frank didn't press the issue, maybe because he had news of his own. "Gallery's openin' a week Saturday."

"How'd ya know that?"

"New sign on the door."

I had to see for myself, so we walked up to Chessman Street. When we got there the entire front of the building was being torn out. Mr. Chambers was swinging a mean sledgehammer.

"Whole front's going to be glass," he told us, answering Frank's question. "Could use your help if you're a mind for a little work."

"How much?" Frank was forever a dreamer, but he was also a businessman.

"You tell me."

The Pranks An' Enlightenment of Frank An' Me

"Twenty cents an hour, each."

"You lads got a union or something?"

Frank made a production of looking around. "Don't see no one else here, Mr. Chambers."

Mr. Chambers laughed. "Nor does I, Frank. Nor does I. Tell you what. You take all this scrap and stuff and load it into my truck and rake up good and I'll pay you fifty cents each. Don't care how long it takes, fifty cents each, is the wage. Then, when you're done with that, if I like the job, another fifty cents, each that is, to help me on the front. I got glass coming on the morning train. So that will be a dollar each, and if we get the glass set in before dark, I'll give you another dollar."

"Each?"

"Each. But I will be the judge of the work. If you slack off or don't follow directions, pay'll be less. Agreed?"

"Agreed!"

Mr. Chambers was a steady worker. He knew exactly what he was doing, shoring up before knocking down, laying lines here and there, and explaining everything as we went along. It didn't seem like work at all, or like learning, which it was, because Mr. Chambers entertained us every step of the way.

About one o'clock he said, "Hold on, boys, you've about tuckered me out. Time for a rest. Mrs. Chambers will be along soon with some food and drink."

"Me an' Frank didn't bring none," I piped up.

"Worry not. I have already called my wife on Mr. Abbey's telephone."

And sure enough, Mrs. Chambers showed up with enough food for six men. She kissed Mr. Chambers coming and going. It was nice to see that affection.

And she greeted Frank and me warmly, inquiring about our health and about our parents and my gran'ma. "'Spect you'll be glad when school starts 'gain. The girls miss it, ya know." She smiled. "Mothers love it when school's in session. That's when we have our vacations."

She didn't stay. I liked Mrs. Chambers even if she wasn't from Smalltown. Mr. Chambers courted her when he was working off-Cape somewhere and married her when she turned sixteen. They had the four girls one right after another.

We were talking with Mr. Chambers when he dropped some news about Mr. Abbey buying up three or four summer cottages out on the Neck for renting to artists.

"Mr. Abbey's spendin' tons o' money." I allowed.

"Seems like it." he said.

"Rumrunnin' money." Frank added.

"Could be. But," said Mr. Chambers, "no one knows. And when Mr. Abbey comes to check the work, for goodness sakes don't say anything."

The gallery opened as promised. A sizable group of people were there, most of them artists, I suppose. Frank and I didn't go, the word getting around that only adults would be welcomed. What we did was look at the painting through the window when no one was about.

Frank looked for the longest time. When I asked him what he was looking for, he said for paintings done by the man who had let him paint that day on the dunes and whose painting had been on the posters.

"Maybe he'll have something next week," Frank said, pointing to the poster on the door which announced the coming of <u>The Most Provocative Artistic Display on Cape Cod</u>.

"Provocative" had been one of our spelling words just last Spring. Frank and I had been in a bit of trouble for using the word. Well, not for using it but for the way we used it.

Spelling words were always given, then we had to look up the meaning and use the words in sentences, just to reinforce the meaning. Frank had started out with "She wore a provocative dress," Miss Beman, our teacher, didn't seem to care for that, but she let it pass. When my turn came, I said, "An' she had a provocative walk." That did it. We had to stay after school and explain what Miss Beman called "our rudeness."

"But I wasn't being rude," I told her. "I kind of like the way some girls walk."

Then Frank piped up with, "I knew it; I should of said bathing suit."

"And what do you think provocative means?" asked Miss Beman.

"Why, excitin', stimulatin', darin', sex ... ."

Miss Beman cut Frank off in mid-sentence. "Well, I never," she shouted. "Your parents will hear about this." With that she fled out the door.

Our parents did hear, the very next day. Ma didn't seem too much concerned but did lecture me about respect and keeping certain thoughts to myself. Frank said his ma just laughed; his pa got all bent out of joint and bawled out Frank for having impure thoughts and for having no regard for Miss Beman's thoughts.

The provocative artistic display was just the first of a rash of Mr. Abbey's gallery shows that got the town upset. But it was the first one that set the tone.

Every day Frank checked the Chessman Street window, hoping to see something by his unnamed artist friend. The gallery was a short walk from his house.

One morning before breakfast he came pounding on our door. Gran'ma was up; Ma and I were still in bed. Gran'ma let Frank in, and he came running to my room, all excited. He had run all the way from the gallery.

"Lord Almighty. Lord Almighty. Get dressed. Ya got ta see it. Hurry. Ya got to see it." He pulled me out of bed. "Come on!"

I tried to stay under the covers. "Where ya want ta go?"

"To the gall'ry! To the gall'ry!"

I got to laughing. He sounded just like Paul Revere yelling "To arms! To arms!" He threw some clothes at me, and of course by this time Ma was up.

"Good gracious, Frank. What's all the ruckus?"

"The gall'ry. Ya got to see the gall'ry." Whatever it was was too much for Frank. He bolted out of the house, headed for the gallery.

I got going as fast as I could. When I got there, there was Frank, nose flattened out against the window. "Look. There's the painting," he shouted.

Sure enough, the painting we had seen on the dune was just inside the window, prominently displayed. Only it wasn't exactly what we had seen. Green sky, red ocean, with what I guessed were sailboats with various colors of sails, but everything was disjointed and there was a lot of other stuff painted in peculiar ways just floating around in the sky. I wasn't sure what I was seeing. I thought I saw a headless woman holding a deer's head, but when I tried to see it clearly, I couldn't see it at all. I saw a banjo clock like Gran'ma had, but then I didn't see it. It was all very confusing to me; Frank couldn't take his eyes off it.

I was losing interest when I saw a painting standing all by itself in the back. It was the Chambers girls, Asturia, Cora, Esther and Bethany, naked as could be!

I knew right off it was the Chambers girls. There was Asturia standing in the middle, tall, stretching out and up, with Cora and Esther on either side and Bethany sitting at Asturia's feet. Asturia had her arms out to the side over her sisters' heads as though she was protecting them.

"Frank! Look!"

"Yah, it's the Chambers girls. I seen it before."

"It's wonderful," I enthused.

"It's okay," Frank offered.

I couldn't take my eyes off the painting, not because the girls were naked but because something else held me, riveted me to the scene. It was the closest I ever came to what later I heard people call a religious experience. Whatever I called it at the time, it was almost otherworldly.

So suddenly that I jumped a foot, a voice said, "Well, at least I have two customers." It was Mr. Abbey.

I started to make some kind of excuse for being there, but Mr. Abbey stopped me. "I'm pleased for your interest, lads. Come on in an' take a look 'round 'fore others come, if there be any others."

Frank made a beeline to his painting. "It is somethin', ain't it," Mr. Abbey said. "Called surrealism an' cubist an' a whole lot of uncomplimentary things by some. Artist's name is Thomas."

Then Mr. Abbey turned to me. "It's called 'Trinity and One,' painted by some unknown artist."

"It's the Chambers girls."

"Oh, couldn't be. The artist don't live anywhere near here."

"Then ya know who painted it?"

"Well, yes, the truth is, I do, but I can't say. But believe me, the artist has never been to Smalltown."

Mr. Abbey gave us a few more minutes, then asked us to leave. "I don't think I've done right by lettin' you boys in," he told us, sweeping his arm toward more nudes. "Probably should say this exhibit is for adults only. But then I guess ain't nothing here you ain't seen before." He ushered us out, thanking us for our interest.

If anyone else saw the Chambers girls in that painting, I don't know who it was, not even Mr. and Mrs. Chambers. But there were considerable comments about some of the nudes, especially the younger ones. Many a summer girl found herself painted and many a parent threw a fit because a daughter had posed in the nude. Too many of them, it turned out, because there was a lot of talk about closing the gallery down, and right after it had opened.

Apparently most of the girls who were supposedly in the paintings protested that they had not posed. There was a big to-do, and it turned out that Mr. Abbey had been slinking about the dunes, photographing people sunbathing in the buff, then taking the pictures, blowing them up, and selling them to his artist friends. The state police got into the action and found some mighty fine cameras and telescopic lenses that brought people right up close.

When it came to the "Trinity and One" painting, Mr. Abbey confessed that he also took a few pictures around town, which, without his saying so, meant that he had been peeking in people's windows.

When all that came out, I finally found out what Mr. Abbey had proposed to Ma, and as it turned out, to some other women as well, namely that they pose for the artists who had rented his cottages on the Neck. Ma thought she was the only one proposed to; she wasn't.

Funny, I never thought of Ma as anything other than my mother. She always looked nice to me, but I never thought she looked like a model, although she was pretty enough in my mind. But posing nude, to this day I can't begin to imagine it.

The gallery was open for only a few weeks. Mr. Abbey was arrested and went to Barnstable court to defend himself.

Frank and I went almost every day to look at "our" paintings. One day Frank's artist was there, trying to get into the gallery.

"Hello, Mr. Thomas," Frank said right off. "Remember me?"

"Indeed I do. You're the boy who paints... ." He paused. "You're the boy who paints the hills."

Frank was pleased as punch that the artist had remembered. "I sure do admire your painting. Come to look at it every chance I get."

"Then, son, you're the only insightful art critic anywhere around here. What's your name?"

The Pranks An' Enlightenment of Frank An' Me

"Frank."

"Frank, because you're the only person who appreciates the painting, I'll tell you what I'm going to do. I'm going to sell that painting to you."

Frank was speechless, almost. He did manage to ask how much the painting cost.

"Five hundred dollars."

Frank gave a terrible groan.

"Five hundred dollars was my asking price. Less to you. Professional discount."

"But Mr. Thomas, I ain't got nothin' like that."

"How much do you have for a painting you like?"

"Nothin'."

"Well, I can't let it go for nothing. I have to get something for it. Tell me honest, how much can you scrape together?"

"Two, three dollars," Frank said, and I wondered where he was going to get that.

"You drive a hard bargain, Frank. One dollar it is, cash. Take it or leave it."

"I'll take it!" Frank lit up like a Christmas tree.

"Hold on; not so fast. There's two conditions. First, I can't get into the gallery. It's been locked by the court, I think. But if you're patient, the painting will be yours. And second, I've got to tell people that I sold it for a lot more. That's to keep up my image as a serious painter."

That settled, I asked Mr. Thomas about the painting I liked.

"No, I don't know the artist," he answered. "If you like the style, it's pretty good. Not my style, though."

When I asked him how much it cost, he said he didn't know, probably a few hundred dollars. Then he added, "It may not be for sale at all. The court may take it, which would be too bad because even if I don't care for it, it's well done."

"But why would the court take it?"

"Evidence against Abbey, assuming he did what people say."

"Did he?"

"I don't know. I'm not into nude painting. Matter of fact, I hardly know Abbey. I put the one painting here to see if there was any market and if there were any real painters in this town. So far the only one I have met is your friend."

The gallery was closed for the five weeks Mr. Abbey was in jail. Obviously he should have served a lot longer than that, but for some reason he didn't, perhaps because he cooperated with the police, although I didn't then and I don't now understand how such blatant invasion of privacy could be ignored. The whole business made for a lot of local publicity and a lot of people went to the gallery.

The gallery closed for the season right after Labor Day and Frank got his painting. When Frank got killed, his parents contacted Mr. Thomas and gave back the painting, not wanting to be reminded of Frank by such an unusual art work. By then Mr. Thomas had achieved some recognition, and the painting was sold to a museum. Mr. Thomas sent Frank's folks five hundred dollars; they kept but one, donating the rest to the school's scholarship fund. Bethany Chambers made use of it years later.

The gallery was opened for two more summers. The next summer was only for local artists, and I guess not too much of the art sold. The third summer brought unpleasant attention to Smalltown again.

The gallery opened that summer with some of the darkest and dullest stuff I ever saw. The artwork was not for sale, but every week Mr. Abbey had an art auction. It was big time. People by the hundreds came just for the Saturday auctions and bid tens of thousands of dollars for a single painting.

I wasn't there, but one Saturday in early August, just as the auction was starting up, the whole place was surrounded by police, Mr. Abbey and some of the people being led away in handcuffs and chains.

They were charged with selling stolen property, the paintings, and for selling worthless copies of other paintings. And I missed the whole affair. I never saw Mr. Abbey again.

But I've gotten ahead of myself. When the gallery closed the first time, I asked Asturia if she had seen the painting. Yes, she said. "My parents took us to see it because they had heard what you said, that the figure looked like me and because you also could see Esther and Cora and Bethany."

"Were it you and your sisters?"

"No, but I thought how beautiful the girls were and wished that it was."

"It didn't bother you that ... the ... naked ... no clothes an' just standing there?"

"No, 'cause it weren't us, and besides, what could you really see? Whatever you saw was in your imagination."

Maybe that was true. I never saw the painting again and now I can't bring it to mind as clearly as I think I saw it back then. Perhaps I didn't see what I think I saw after all; maybe it was just because I was innocent and impressionable; maybe it was because it was a kind of beauty I'd never seen; maybe I saw only what I wanted to see, just as Frank saw in his painting whatever it was he wanted to see.

Robert Wolley

An' Finally

The Pranks An' Enlightenment of Frank An' Me

Some time ago, while repairing a wooden screen door, I got to thinking that I'd been repairing doors and such ever since Pa left, repairing being a value of thrift taught me a long time back because Pa never did provide for Ma and me once he drove away in the other lady's Buick.

You might ask why, in this day and age, anyone would have a wooden screen door: it warps; it needs paint; sometimes it binds. Aluminum doors don't warp, don't need to be painted, don't bind. And this is my answer: aluminum doors don't have the distinctive "ring" of a wooden door when they bang shut.

When I built my present house, I wanted the sound of a wooden door closing, the sound I remember almost from the day I was born. It may only be sentimental nostalgia, but in that sound I hear memories: of lessons learned, of courage, of community, of caring, and I draw strength from the memories.

Mostly, I hear memories of Frank and me.

During all the years that screen door has been closing, I've heard the memories, and throughout the years, I've told myself I ought to write them down. And when I was repairing the door the last time, I began to compose stories about Frank and me and the people who populated our little world in the time leading to the Great Depression and during it and ending with Frank's death at the beginning of World War II.

I figured, too, that I should set down the facts before somebody else came along and told them differently. No doubt there will be those who will wonder how I could let my imagination run so wild. Of course, the people I have told about are gone, so you have to believe me, don't you?

One thing Frank and I didn't know at the time of our growing up was that we, meaning everyone around us, were "characters" because of our distinctive, usually meaning peculiar, traits.

Frank would have loved that epithet, would have said that it gave him style. But Frank didn't need such a label. He was endowed with a flair for life, what we used to "verve." He had a knack for making life comical, even when to others it might have seemed absurd.

With Frank went the last vestige of childhood, forecast, it seems in retrospect, with Gran'ma's death. Neither would have tolerated any darkness; life was too full of sunshine for regrets.

Even when Frank and I were in business, we treated the whole affair as just another mad adventure and enjoyed every minute of it. It is that sure, pure joy of living I wanted to tell. If you don't believe anything else about Frank an' me, believe that we enjoyed just being alive, because that's the truth.

Gran'ma used to recite little versus and sing short verse-songs to me now and then. One I remember she had all wrong, although her heart was pure. I looked it up once and found the proper wording. It seems to end these stories fittingly. It was written a long time ago by a man named Herman Neuman:

> *Two chambers has the heart,*
> *Wherein dwell Joy and Sorrow;*
> *When Joy awakes in one,*
> *Then slumbers Sorrow in the other.*
> *O Joy, take care!*
> *Speak softly,*
> *Lest you awaken Sorrow.*
>
> *from* <u>The Heart</u>